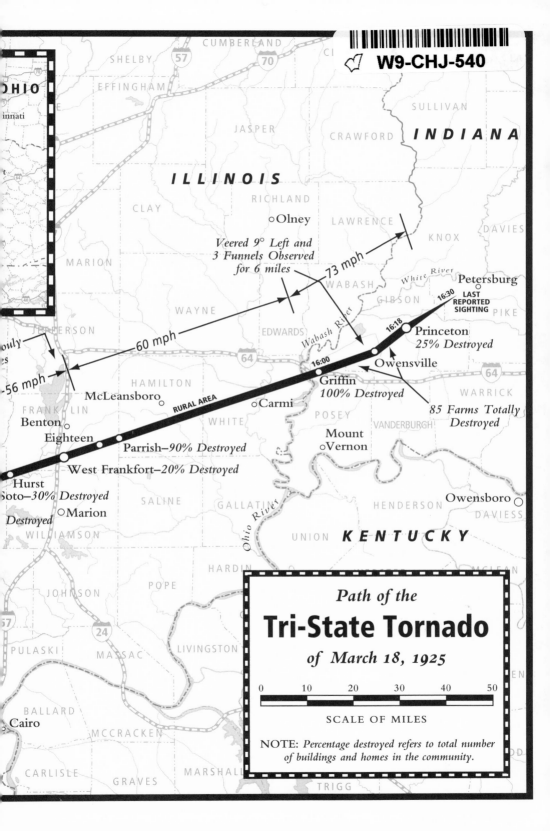

OHIO

innati

SHELBY

EFFINGHAM

CUMBERLAND

JASPER

CRAWFORD

SULLIVAN

INDIANA

ILLINOIS

CLAY

RICHLAND

Olney

LAWRENCE

KNOX

DAVIES

MARION

WAYNE

*Veered 9° Left and
3 Funnels Observed
for 6 miles*

White River

Petersburg

GIBSON

PIKE

16:30

LAST
REPORTED
SIGHTING

73 mph

WABASH

Wabash River

EDWARDS

16:18

Princeton
25% Destroyed

JEFFERSON

60 mph

64

16:00

Owensville

ouly
es

56 mph

HAMILTON

RURAL AREA

McLeansboro

Carmi

Griffin
100% Destroyed

POSEY

WARRICK

64

FRANKLIN

WHITE

VANDERBURGH

*85 Farms Totally
Destroyed*

Benton

Eighteen

Parrish–90% Destroyed

Mount
Vernon

Hurst

West Frankfort–20% Destroyed

SALINE

GALLATIN

Ohio River

HENDERSON

Owensboro

DAVIESS

Soto–30% Destroyed

Marion

Destroyed

WILLIAMSON

UNION

KENTUCKY

HARDIN

JOHNSON

POPE

PULASKI

MASSAC

LIVINGSTON

24

BALLARD

Cairo

MCCRACKEN

CARLISLE

GRAVES

MARSHALL

TRIGG

Path of the
Tri-State Tornado
of March 18, 1925

| 0 | 10 | 20 | 30 | 40 | 50 |

SCALE OF MILES

NOTE: *Percentage destroyed refers to total number
of buildings and homes in the community.*

THE FORGOTTEN STORM

THE FORGOTTEN STORM

The Great Tri-State Tornado of 1925

WALLACE AKIN

The Lyons Press

Guilford, Connecticut

An Imprint of The Globe Pequot Press

The Lyons Press is an imprint of The Globe Pequot Press

Printed in the United States of America

10 9 8 7 6 5 4 3 2 1

Design by Paul L. Schiff

Library of Congress Cataloging-in-Publication data is available on file.

DEDICATION

To all those who died in the great storm
and to all those who survived to tell the tale.

CONTENTS

LIST OF MAPS AND FIGURES

Acknowledgements

Many thanks to Noah Lukeman, my agent, who was the first to encourage me to write this book, and also to Ann Treistman, my editor, who kept me focused on the tornado when I wandered too far afield into local history.

The Interlibrary Loan department at Cowles Library of Drake University never failed to assist me, nor did the many anonymous librarians who searched their holdings seeking microfilm of newspapers from cities and towns throughout the area. Historical societies have been very helpful: the Indiana Historical Society and the Indiana State Library supplied valuable microfilm. Special thanks to Robert Morefield, curator of photographs for the Jackson County Historical Society in Murphysboro.

Many journalists who entered the devastated storm areas wrote vivid accounts of the destruction and stories of the survivors. I thank them and the newspaper profession for retaining so much historic material and for their generosity in sharing it. Particularly valuable to me were the archives of the *St. Louis Post-Dispatch* and *Globe Democrat*—newspapers that I delivered to subscribers throughout much of my boyhood in Murphysboro—and also the *Chicago Tribune*, and the *Murphysboro Daily Independent*.

When I first began my research, I realized this treasure-trove of newspaper accounts would be important to my story. This book is based on facts as reported in these news stories, and on my own meteorological knowledge and my experience growing up in the storm-affected area, aware of all the cultural nuances. Minor enhancements were necessary when presenting some accounts, but only to add details based on my personal knowledge. Direct quotations are intact and credited, minor exceptions explained.

I am grateful to all those who fed my childhood memory bank with the great tornado lore, and especially to my mother whose courage and quick action saved my life during the great storm. My immediate family has supported me throughout—Dianna, David, thanks to you both. A special thanks to my wife, Peggy, who not only encouraged me to write this book; she helped me write it.

INTRODUCTION

My grandmother was a superstitious woman who was forever looking for "signs," and she was inclined to make predictions based on them. When I was very young I believed she was clairvoyant, a wizard who knew everything. But as I grew older I came to realize that her predictions were as likely to miss the mark as to hit it. When I questioned her about her failures she was never the least perturbed, always offering what seemed to her to be a logical explanation.

Her specialty was cloud-watching and predictions about the weather; these were the ones most likely to hit the mark, and they certainly were far more interesting to me than the official weather forecasts from the radio or newspaper. For instance, if we were sitting on her porch on a moonlit summer night my grandmother might say, "Do you see that circle around the moon, Wallace? I see three stars inside it. We should have rain in three days." (Although she was unaware of it, circles around the moon are created by light refraction from ice crystals in a high cirrus veil, indicating the advance of warm moist air aloft and rain might well develop later from such a set-up.) Or she might say, "See that smoke floating west? Look for rain tomorrow." (An east wind often does indicate the approach of a warm front and rain.)

My grandmother took pride in the fact that she had predicted the great storm of 1925. That morning she had remarked to my mother, "Too warm for March. A bad storm is on the way. Those frogs will be looking through glass windows by morning." In our local pond the frogs always came to life with the first warm spell and entertained the whole neighborhood with a great choral symphony, celebrating the end of *their winter hibernation with croaking that ranged from soprano to basso profundo.*

That day my grandmother was prophetic. Even as she uttered those words, a very bad storm indeed was on its way: at approximately 1:03 in the afternoon of March 18, 1925, the Tri-State Tornado made its debut in the Ozarks of southeastern Missouri. Once on the ground this great tornado set records against which we still measure all others—in its death toll, length of track, forward speed, and duration. Its first casualty was a farmer, the first of 695 people who would perish before it ran its course as it cut an uninterrupted 219-mile swath through three states—southeastern Missouri, southern Illinois, and southwestern Indiana. A quarter-mile wide in the beginning, it grew dramatically to a width of nearly one mile during most of its three and-a-half-hour run. Its forward speed varied throughout the afternoon from fifty-six miles per hour to an astounding seventy-three miles per hour—more than twice the speed of an average tornado.

My hometown, Murphysboro, Illinois, only twelve miles east of the Mississippi River, was worst hit. When the tornado roared through, it picked up houses as if they were toys. My mother crouched in one of them, clutching me: I was only two years old at the time. On that memorable day every member of my family suffered trauma, and even though we all survived, that one minute in time remained a defining moment for the rest of our lives.

Perhaps it is not surprising that for me the sky has always been a mysterious place where the unexpected lurked, and I grew up acutely aware of its power and its whims—to destroy crops or to save them, to impose terrible summer heat waves and also to dispel them with spectacular thunderstorms and torrents of rain that soaked me to the skin before I could deliver all my newspapers. And like everyone in Murphysboro I knew all too well its power to kill. Like my grandmother, I learned to watch the sky for signs, not so much from fear as from fascination.

At the beginning of a new millennium, in this last chapter of my life, I seem to have come full circle, caught up once more in the awesome power of that great event which so shaped my life. I return to the scenes of my early years, growing up in the aftermath of the great storm that is all but forgotten even by many professional meteorologists. It is my privilege to share its story and perhaps to help return it to its rightful place as one of the nation's great natural disasters.

The Fujita Scale of Tornado Destruction

F0	Weak tornado (40-72 mph; 54-116 kmph)	Light damage: Shingles removed from roofs; tree limbs broken; signs downed.
F1	Moderate tornado (73-112 mph; 117-180 kmph)	Moderate damage: Parts of roof missing; overturned mobile homes; shallow-rooted trees toppled.
F2	Significant tornado (113-157 mph; 182-253 kmph)	Considerable damage: Most of roof missing from well-constructed house; mobile homes obliderated; automobiles overturned; well-constructed barns demolished.
F3	Severe tornado (158-206 mph; 254-332 kmph)	Severe damage: Removes roofs and outer walls of well-constructed houses; autos blown for many yards.
F4	Devastating tornado (207-260 mph; 333-418 kmph)	Devastating damage: Well-built houses completely demolished; automobiles, buses, and farm machinery carried hundred of yards; well-rooted trees completely stripped of bark and branches or toppled.
F5	Incredible tornado (261-318 mph; 420-512 kmph)	Incredible damage: Strong, well-constructed houses obliterated and debris scattered—empty foundations are F5 trademarks.
F6	Tornadoes in this range cannot possibly exist.	Damage inconceivable: If such tornadoes ever occur, damage will be indistinguishable from that of F5.

The late Professor T. Theodore Fujita of the University of Chicago developed this classification system known as the F-scale. The National Weather Service and weather services worldwide use it as the basis for evaluating storm damage from tornadoes and downbursts. It is far from perfect because, although it includes estimated wind velocities that produce the damage, it does not take into account variations in building construction when the damage is assessed, nor does it measure storms that cause no structural damage; thus, it is not applicable to tornadoes or downbursts in open country. Unquestionably, along most of its path, the Tri-State Tornado met the test of an F5 rating.

CHAPTER 1

WITHOUT WARNING

NO ONE CLAIMED to have seen the initial touchdown on that gray day. The first known eyewitness was a rural mail carrier making his rounds about four miles north of the little Ozark town of Ellington in the rugged hill country of Reynolds County, Missouri. As his horse-drawn mail cart—a high-wheeled enclosed box—lurched along the country road and came over a rise, directly ahead, blocking his path and towering over the valley beyond, a broad purple blackness hovered. Within it he heard "a great commotion" and saw a funnel extended downward, moving gracefully across the hills. Reining in his horse, he watched as trees and debris tumbled high in the air, carried aloft in the twisting pillar of wind, while at ground level a cloud of dust and fog obscured its base. He stared mesmerized until it disappeared heading northeast across Logan's Creek.

Word of his sighting, however, did not reach those who lived farther east along the tornado's path. In 1925 the U.S. Weather Bureau had no tornado warning system in place. All along the storm's route, people went about their daily tasks unaware of what was bearing down upon them. And because of its tremendous speed, those who did see it coming had little time to seek shelter. Daily newspapers did print weather forecasts, and radios repeated them, but few people owned radios and few in rural areas read daily newspapers. In any case, at that time official weather forecasts were of little value. The evening before the tragedy these mundane forecasts appeared:

MISSOURI: Showers probable tonight and Wednesday; colder Wednesday. *(St. Louis Post-Dispatch)*

ILLINOIS: Rain probable tonight or Wednesday; colder Wednesday or Wednesday night. *(St. Louis Post-Dispatch)*

INDIANA: Mostly overcast Tuesday and Wednesday; probably showers by Tuesday night; moderate temperature. *(Chicago Tribune)*

Even as these forecasts were being written, the already developed cyclonic system was moving inexorably across the dry plains of Oklahoma, entering the area north of the Gulf of Mexico, setting the stage for the development of tornadoes that would make March 18, 1925 the most deadly tornado day in American history. By 1:00 P.M. the storm's low center hovered over southeastern Missouri and southwestern Illinois. Eighty miles southwest of the storm's center, behind the cold front of the system, a supercell thunderstorm (a phenomenon then unrecognized by forecasters) had formed over the Missouri Ozarks. From out of this supercell was born the super tornado that killed and injured so many.

That evening of March 18, the Weather Bureau's Chicago office sent a summary of the day's weather to area newspapers:

The storm, which was centered on the southern Great Plains Tuesday, has since developed considerably in intensity and moved directly northeastward, the center Wednesday evening being astride the Ohio valley. The area of precipitation on Wednesday reached from the lower Missouri and middle Mississippi valleys eastward across the Appalachian mountain region, snow falling in the northern portion of the area, and rain, accompanied by thunderstorms, in the southern and central portions. The attendant winds moreover, have been fresh to strong, and severe squalls have occurred in localities.

That was all: fresh to strong shifting winds, rain, unsettled conditions, severe squalls. In reality, nine tornadoes, one of unsurpassed dimensions, had occurred as the storm system moved across the eastern United States, yet the U.S. Weather Bureau officially refused to acknowledge them. Accustomed as we now are to constant media weather coverage and instant replays, this failure seems a dereliction of duty, but without a doubt observers in Weather Bureau offices in St. Louis and Chicago had suspected violent weather was a possibility when they issued their forecasts. Certainly by the time they posted that evening report stating that the storm center had moved on they were aware of the day's disasters. Why did they fail to forecast and report realistically? The answer lies in the official regulations of the time. In 1925, the U.S. Weather Bureau forbade government meteorologists to use "tornado" in forecasts or in official reports, fearing such scare words might alarm citizens and curtail the general flow of commerce. The word "tornado" appeared only in summaries published months after the severe weather occurred.

This restriction had not always been in effect. As early as the 1880s successful tornado forecasting was evolving under the direc-

3

tion of Lieutenant John Park Finley of the U.S. Army Signal Corps, but General Adolphus Greely, new chief of the Corps, put an end to this research in 1887 although he realized the danger from tornadoes. He banned the word "tornado" in public forecasts, reasoning that the exact point of touchdown could not be predicted (even today exact predictions are not possible). Finley, moved to a new post with the Signal Corps, continued his interest in tornadoes but his research into tornado forecasting came to an end. For many years, General Greely's ban remained. Writing in the Weather Bureau's *Monthly Weather Review,* in April of 1925, the editor summarized the prevailing ignorance: "it must be reluctantly admitted that there is little hope that the actual conditions that initiate a tornado vortex will ever be experimentally observed."[1]

In 1891, weather forecasting and research moved from the Army Signal Corps to the Department of Agriculture, shifting control from military to civilian authority. The Weather Bureau officially became established. This was in recognition of the importance of weather to farming and an acknowledgment that most scientists working in that field were civilians. Nevertheless, the ban against tornado forecasting remained in effect until 1952.

The Weather Bureau finally lifted the ban after two pioneer meteorologists proved the possibility of forecasting a tornado and the media gave wide publicity to their success. The ensuing public outcry for reform forced the Bureau to take notice. On March 25, 1948, the two scientists, Major Ernest Fawbush and Captain Robert Miller, assigned to Tinker Air Force Base near Oklahoma City, made their remarkable forecast based on years of studying weather conditions preceding and accompanying tornadoes. (Although they had more sophisticated instrumentation and data, they used the same empirical approach that Finley had used in the 1880s.) They went out on a limb, predicting tornadoes in central Oklahoma for that very day. Since the base had suffered tornado damage only five days earlier, the commanding officer took no chances and all hands rushed to secure the facility. (Although Fawbush and Miller had predicted the earlier storm, they had not told anyone, but with confirmation that their method worked, they announced their March 25 forecast to other air force personnel.)

At 6:00 P.M. that day, out of a low-hanging black cloud, a tornado touched down directly on Tinker Air Base—two tornadoes within five days, rare indeed! After the story came out and Bureau resistance crumbled, tornado forecasting, using Fawbush and Miller's method, became standard along with a warning system. The public received their first forecast of a tornado possibility on March 17, 1952, twenty-seven years almost to the day after the Tri-State disaster.[2]

If my family had received an early tornado warning that day in 1925, we might have been spared some hardship. My father owned an automobile dealership and repair shop near downtown; he was caught outside unaware. My eighteen-year-old brother, who worked inside the shop crawled out when the shop fell; he set off in search of our father and found him unconscious, with a horrendous, near-fatal head injury.

My father was nearly forty years old then and he had recently invested all his savings and hopes in his business. A shipment of new cars had just arrived, and he hastened to insure them. On the day of the tornado he had placed in his jacket pocket a letter to that effect along with a signed form and a check for the premium. The letter was never mailed, never found. It was gone with the wind along with his major investment. After he recovered from his injury the business had to be rebuilt from the ground up. Insurance covered the building; the demolished cars were his heavy debt to bear. But his situation differed little from that of other townspeople. With 70 percent of Murphysboro's homes destroyed or severely damaged and 40 percent of the entire town gone, scarcely a family remained untouched.

Even the Great Depression, which hit the town just four years after the storm, failed to equal the pain of that event. Genteel poverty can be tolerable when all share the privations and hope for better days, but the death of so many in one horrible minute, especially the many children, and the violent destruction of property, seemed to leave a permanent pall over the town.

Storm phobia was prevalent among survivors for many decades. With every spring and summer storm, every crash of thunder and every bank of black clouds appearing over the horizon, many of these survivors headed toward newly-built storm cellars. Lightning and violent wind during the night was especially frightening. I recall such nights when, roused from sleep, I hurried over to wake my grandmother, while my parents hastily dressed for our visit to the neighborhood storm cellar. My grandmother, wide awake, invariably waited for me by her front door carrying her Bible, the family photograph album, and a sack of snack food for me.

Vacant lots, steps leading nowhere, and junk-filled basements exposed to the elements, these gaping wounds remained visible in the town for many years. We found no lack of places to play. Empty basements in particular made inviting forts, and many vacant lots became subsistence gardens for our parents.

The phantom of the Tri-State Tornado even followed me out of town. When I graduated from high school I enrolled in the university at Carbondale, a mere seven miles from home. One of the first things I did was seek a campus job, and it just seemed natural to choose one that obligated me to trek over to the weather instrument shelter every six hours, record the barometric pressure and temperature, check the rain gauge, and call in the readings to an airline headquarters in Denver.

By good fortune my supervisor happened to be chairman of the geography department and teacher of weather and climate: the affable Thomas F. Barton. "Where are you from?" was the first question he asked. The second was, "Were you living there during the tornado?" Straight away, he invited me to sign up for his class, and just like that, I found my mentor and a lifelong friend.

The Second World War interrupted my education at Carbondale. Four years in the Navy gave me an opportunity to study meteorology at Columbia University Midshipman School. Afterward, I experienced two other violent acts of nature, a hurricane on land near Chesapeake Bay and a typhoon at sea in the Western Pacific.[3] The latter we managed to ride out in a small wooden mine sweeper. As commanding officer, I had constantly to monitor changing weather conditions—mostly tropical—with which we had to cope.

Later, as a graduate student, I joined Tom Barton at Indiana University. On my first day the department chairman asked apologetically if I minded sharing an office with their eccentric professor, Ronald Ives. The chairman warned me forthrightly—Professor Ives could be difficult. He was also a brilliant teacher of physical geography, specializing in weather and climate. We got along famously and again the Tri-State Tornado played its part. Because of his great interest in all severe storms, especially tornadoes and hurricanes, he seemed pleased to share his office with a survivor of such an historic weather event, and he tutored me in the meteorology of all those violent phenomena of nature. When I finished my study there I continued with my doctoral work at Northwestern University and finally embarked on my own teaching career where weather was and remains a specialty in my professional life.

While the story of the Tri-State Tornado has historic value, it can also serve as a warning for those who have never experienced such storms and are unaware of how deadly they can be. I, as do most scientists, believe that global warming is increasing the frequency of severe storms, and this is a subject little understood by the public and their elected officials, who tend to focus only on temperature changes. But it is about more than just warming. Our gluttony for energy is loading the atmosphere with pollutants and increasing the greenhouse effect. This subject is far too complicated to discuss briefly, but be assured that we can expect more frequent and more violent acts of nature, more hurricanes, more heavy deluges of rain with resultant floods and mud slides—and more frequent supertornadoes.

CHAPTER 2

Nature Sets the Stage

A TORNADO OF THE MAGNITUDE of the Tri-State would never have occurred in most other parts of the world. Only in Bangladesh have storms rivaled its deadliness, but not its magnitude. It took the unique geography of the central United States, combined with extraordinary weather conditions dependent on this geography—an unusually strong jet stream aloft, the presence of warm, moist tropical air on the surface, and the development of the vast supercell thunderstorm near the center of the parent cyclone—to cause such a storm.

Unlike Europe, Asia, and North Africa, where major mountain ranges run east and west, North America features broad prairies, forests, and fields that lie within a thousand-mile wide natural passageway bordered by mountain ranges that run north and south: the Rocky Mountains in the west and the Appalachians in the east. At the southern end of this corridor the Gulf of Mexico lies in a great saucer-shaped embayment, extending the warm waters of the tropical Atlantic 1,100 miles westward beyond the 97th meridian. Within this vast corridor between the tropics and the polar regions there are no significant topographic barriers.[1] Weatherwise, this is of enormous importance, since air of tropical and polar continental origins can move unimpeded by terrain. When, along this vast stretch, warm moist tropical air masses from the Gulf of Mexico meet the cold, dry air from the continental interior, violent thunderstorms and tornadoes can form, particularly when aided by an inflow aloft of warm, dry air from the semiarid and arid lands farther west. The great Tri-State Tornado of 1925 developed from such a clash, but only extraordinary atmospheric conditions could have generated its astonishing forward speed and longevity.

Tornadoes are most frequent in the spring, when temperature contrasts between the opposing air masses are greatest, but they are storms for all seasons. Fortunately, most clashes between warm and cold air do not produce tornadoes; other atmospheric conditions, many still not understood, must also be present. As the earth warms in the southern part of the passageway, some of this solar energy heats the air above the surface, and some of it evaporates water and becomes locked in the warm air as latent heat of vaporization. Wind transports this latent heat inland. When released by condensation, it warms the air and contributes to instability. Meanwhile, the northern air remains cold from its contact with the frozen soil. Like oil and water, warm and cold air will not mix.

*   *   *

In 1925, ships crossing the Gulf of Alaska bound for Anchorage reported a drop in pressure indicating a low that lasted from the thirteenth to the eighteenth of March. The cyclonic storm within which the Tri-State Tornado later developed was an offshoot of this low. It must have separated from this parent low-pressure area to become a separate storm system on about 13 March.

Middle latitude cyclones are low pressure areas indicated by closed isobars surrounding them on weather maps. They move downstream in the Westerlies. These great atmospheric depressions cover many thousands of square miles and can be well over 1,000 miles across. Outside the tropics these cyclonic systems usually involve at least two contrasting air masses—one cold and one warm—separated by fronts. Where cold air is advancing within a system it under runs the lighter warm air forcing it aloft along a cold front; where warm air is the aggressor it displaces cold air at the surface and rises over it along a warm front that marks its leading edge at the surface. It is within these larger systems that tornadoes develop if conditions are present—usually in advance of a cold front or a warm front. The Tri-State Tornado formed within the system after the cyclone reached a position north of the Gulf of Mexico and the nature of the air in the warm sector changed.

* * *

Going ashore from the Gulf, the new cyclone moved southeastward across the fjords and islands of the Alaskan panhandle, following the orientation of the polar jet stream above, which now had turned southeast across the mountains of western Canada. Winds there circulated around the low in a counterclockwise spiral in response to the earth's rotation.

North of the storm's track, easterly winds from the plains of northern Canada brought clear, cold weather to southern Alaska, while moist Pacific maritime air from the west flowed south of the low. Forced upward by the forest-clad terrain of the islands and the Coast Mountains, this maritime air cooled and gave up copious quantities of its moisture, which created fog, low stratus clouds, and rain.

The Alaskan panhandle is a land of spectacular scenery. It is mountainous in the extreme with precipitous slopes leading to scores of peaks with elevations above 5,000 feet, and some are 10,000 to 15,000 feet high. Innumerable bays, tidewater inlets, many islands, and steep fjords (some with huge glaciers descending to the sea) cut the land. Trees grow on these steep slopes up to elevations of 1,000 to 3,000 feet.

Storms constantly move inland from the Gulf of Alaska bringing almost daily rains to this coast. Despite the high latitude of the panhandle, heavy rainfall and above-freezing winter temperatures produce a benign marine climate that favored the growth of a rainforest. This once great forest was decimated by commercial logging. Today, remnants of it are preserved in the towering cedars, hemlocks, and Sitka spruce of the Tongass National Forest.

Crossing the Coast Range, the path of the cyclone gradually curved southeast where it passed over the Canadian province of British Columbia and crossed the Canadian Rocky Mountains into Alberta, perhaps bringing some snow to the scenic Jasper and Banff National Parks that lie along the eastern slope of the mountains with their magnificent alpine scenery, rugged snow-capped peaks, precipitous flat-floored glacial valleys, and beautiful waterfalls that spill into them.

Up to this point on the cyclone's long journey its exact route is just an educated guess, but from here on weather observers in Canada and the United States kept a careful record of its movement.

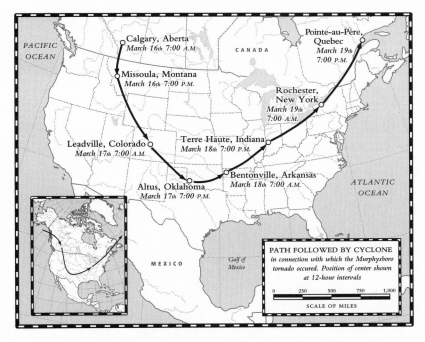

The path followed by the parent cyclonic storm that spawned the Tri-State Tornado over the southeastern Missouri Ozarks. Weather station locations show positions of the low-pressure center at twelve-hour intervals. The jet stream probably followed approximately the same path. Modified from an original map compiled in 1925 by Lee Yoder from six hourly maps published by the U.S. Weather Bureau for March 16th through 19th.

The low center and the weather accompanying it first appeared on Canadian weather maps the morning of March 16, when it centered near Calgary, Alberta. From there, it moved almost due south some 346 miles, traveling about twenty-nine miles per hour. It reached Missoula, Montana at 7:00 P.M., its first appearance on United States Weather Bureau maps.

So gradual were changes in wind direction as the low traveled southward along the crest of the Rocky Mountains that wind-shift lines (where wind direction changes abruptly as along a cold front) did not appear until much farther along its track.[2]

*   *   *

Discovering the Jet Stream

In 1925, meteorologists were not aware of the jet stream, a corridor of rapidly moving air some 35,000 to 40,000 feet above the sur-

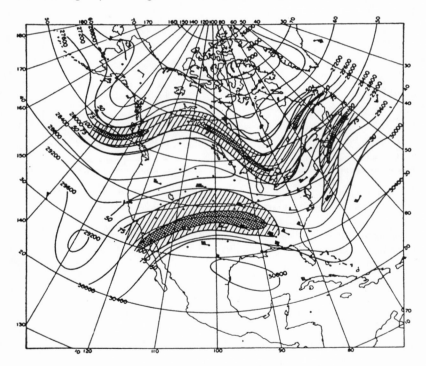

The pressure and winds aloft over North America on October 25, 1950. Two jet streams are well developed between 27,000 and 30,400 feet at the 300-millibar level. The Polar Jet (sometimes called the Subpolar Jet) lies north of the Canadian border and the subtropical jet crosses the southern United States. Hatched areas indicate regions where wind speed exceeds 75 knots (86 mph); in the crosshatched areas winds exceeded 100 knots (115 mph). One Rosby wave crest lies over Alaska, one over Western Canada, and one over the Maritime Provinces of Canada. (Source: Air Force Manual 105-5, Weather for Aircrew Trainees, 1956).

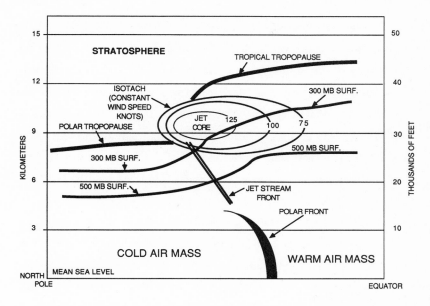

A schematic cross-section of a Polar Jet Stream looking eastward or downstream. The horizontal scale of the diagram is greatly exaggerated. (Modified from Air Force Manual 105-5).

face. It was not until World War II that Japanese scientists discovered it while experimenting with balloons intended to float incendiary devices across the Pacific Ocean to North America. Although the experiment failed, their discovery of the jet stream made a significant contribution to meteorology. Only a few months later American atmospheric scientists independently stumbled onto the jet when bombers returning to bases south of Japan ran out of fuel because of unsuspected headwinds. These unfortunate pilots had inadvertently flown into the strong river of air flowing northeastward toward Japan.

*   *   *

Throughout the night of March 16, the storm center continued southeastward, accelerating to fifty-four miles per hour. Entering Wyoming near Yellowstone Park it moved along the continental divide, arriving at Leadville, Colorado at 7:00 A.M. on the seventeenth. Again, very little weather accompanied it. Leadville reported only a half-inch of precipitation, although greater amounts may have fallen as snow on the higher slopes of the Rocky Mountains.[3]

Colorado and the southern Rocky Mountains, unlike western Montana, reported below average snowfall for the winter of 1924-1925, resulting in a shortage of irrigation water from snowmelt the following summer. The fact that this cyclone produced little precipitation to the water-deprived areas of the West explains why it made little impression on weather observers—it was just another cyclonic system which, like so many others that winter, did little to alleviate the drought.

On March 17, the cyclone left the southern Colorado mountains and entered the vast Great Plains, which lie mostly west of the one hundredth meridian. These plains stretch eastward toward an indefinite boundary with the central lowlands of the United States. Its outstanding feature is its dry climate that sets it apart from the humid East. Rainfall here averages less than twenty inches per year; during droughts, it can be very dry indeed, in many years receiving less than ten inches of precipitation. The dry weather of 1925 was but a harbinger of the great drought and "Dust Bowl" to follow.

It is not surprising that this parent cyclone did little to alleviate the drought conditions of the southern Great Plains. A cyclonic system causes flow into it from surrounding areas and the nature of this air changes as the system moves cross-country. At this point in its path, the Rocky Mountains were an effective block to moisture from the Pacific Ocean; to the south lay the high, dry plains of Texas, New Mexico, and Arizona, and farther south the dry plateaus of northern Mexico. With no significant source of moist air to feed the cyclonic system, neither rain nor snow fell.

*   *   *

Continuing southeast, the cyclonic system crossed the northeastern corner of New Mexico and the Texas panhandle gradually moving toward a more easterly track, the center reaching the town of Altus in the southwestern corner of Oklahoma at 7:00 P.M. steered by the jet. The system's forward motion was slowing, and again much-needed rain failed to fall.

During the next twelve hours the central low crossed Oklahoma, gradually curving first to the east and then northeast. It had left the dry western plains and passed into the humid East where it was now north of the western shore of the Gulf of Mexico. (The humid-dry boundary in North America extends northward from the point where it intersects the Gulf Coast just north of the mouth of the Rio Grande.)

East of Tulsa the center of the cyclonic system left Oklahoma and headed northeast on an undeviating course. By the time it reached Arkansas, near Bentonville, at 7:00 A.M. on March 18, the nature of its component air masses had changed. Up to this point in the life of the storm, there had been nothing to indicate the violent weather it would spawn in the eastern part of its journey, but now the central low was north of the Gulf of Mexico and, at last, a strong flow of moist air was moving northward ahead of the low pressure center. A warm front extended southeastward from the low center, marking the leading edge of this stream of Gulf air. North of this front the warm air was overriding the cooler surface air and it shifted counterclockwise in a cyclonic swirl, flowing in behind the low center. At the surface, cool, dry air from the north slipped southeast under this warm air in the western quadrant of the storm. Its leading edge formed a cold front that extended south from the storm center. In the vernacular of the 1920s, it was now a well-established "wind-shift line."

All the ingredients for severe weather were in place: a well-defined low level jet was at the core of the warm air flowing northward to the east of the cold front. This cold front formed a sharp boundary between the cold air mass from the north and the warm, tropical maritime air. Aloft, this overriding warm, moist air was swinging around counterclockwise behind the low, and capping this warm air was a layer of warm, dry air moving in from the southwest.[4] Over all this, more unstable cold air extended upward to the *tropopause,* the lower boundary of the stratosphere. Just below the stratosphere the rapidly moving polar jet served as a ventilating mechanism above the storm and propelled the surface cyclone eastward.

In a typical tornado model, this warm, dry layer, like the lid of a pressure cooker, traps moist warm air below. If the warm air receives enough lift to break through this warmer capping layer it penetrates the cold, unstable level above, and its upward motion accelerates; expansion, cooling, and condensation occur, and towering cumulonimbus clouds form. On March 18, 1925, all these contributing factors played their part; severe weather was imminent.

From Bentonville, the low moved northeastward across southern Missouri. As in areas farther west, the Ozark plateau of the southwestern part of the state had been suffering the driest March on record. The cyclone on the eighteenth brought little or no rain to its southern margins until the Tri-State's parent supercell thunderstorm developed.

North of the storm's path was another story. Once the storm reached a position north of the Gulf of Mexico, it created a pressure gradient that facilitated the northward flow of a vast tongue of warm air, and thunderstorms broke out from southeastern Kansas and across west central Missouri. Weather stations lying between thirty and sixty miles north of the center's track reported heavy rainfall on the eighteenth, mostly from thunderstorms, which accounted for as much as 90 percent of the month's total rain.

In the early morning hours of March 18, an F2 tornado touched down near Dearing, Kansas, just north of the Oklahoma border. It destroyed a gas station and a barn, and it damaged several houses. It was the first of nine tornadoes that would form that day as the cyclonic system moved eastward. Shortly before 1:00 P.M. the storm center hovered over the Mississippi River about seventy miles southeast of St. Louis. Eighty miles behind it the supercell thunderstorm that spawned the Tri-State Tornado formed over Reynolds County, Missouri, in the cold-air sector of the cyclonic system. This was a very unusual position because the typical supercell develops ahead of the cold front in the warm-air sector of a cyclone. A strong cyclonic circulation, the proximity to the low center, a layer of warm air aloft, and a vigorous jet above provided the environment for maximum thunderstorm growth and tornado development over the eastern Ozarks.

*   *   *

The Supercell Thunderstorm

Before 1962, the term *supercell* did not appear in the vocabulary of meteorologists. Frank Ludlum and Keith Browning were the first to describe a supercell after they observed a massive thunderstorm that crossed the English Channel from France into southern England on July 9, 1959. The word itself first appeared in a professional paper written by Browning in 1962.[5] Along its 130-mile-long path, that giant thunderstorm pelted the British land with hail that reached the size of baseballs in the town of Workingham. Meteorologists Ludlum and Browning used five radar units with the input of "ground truth" by more than 2,000 volunteer observers in southern England. Radar made it possible for them to study the airflow patterns within the storm.[6]

Most supercell thunderstorms are five to ten miles across, but some may exceed twenty miles. They are part of a larger cyclonic system with well-defined fronts between moist tropical air and air of polar origin. A supercell thunderstorm may contain secondary warm and cold fronts and a tightly rotating wind pattern. These mini-systems, called mesocyclones, (almost always present when tornadoes occur) help supercells maintain their identity for many hours as they move across country, spreading destruction not only from tornadoes but from violent downbursts. Downpours of rain and hailstorms often accompany them and they sometimes bring flash floods.

*　　*　　*

Shortly before 1:00 P.M. a massive supercell thunderstorm towered over the hills and valleys of southeastern Missouri, about to give birth to the most deadly American tornado of record. Had the field of meteorology progressed steadily from its early promise in the late nineteenth century, forecasters might have been able to recognize the many factors that contributed to the development and longevity of this tornado, and they might have had in place a warning system. Unfortunately, such warnings were not there.

CHAPTER 3

TOUCHDOWN IN MISSOURI

IN SOUTHEASTERN MISSOURI the day was unusually warm for mid-March, about 65°F. The steep wooded slopes of the Courtois Hills were adorned with flowering redbuds weeks ahead of schedule. They seemed to have blossomed overnight, forming a colorful understory beneath the canopy of oaks and pines. The rose-purple flowers, pressed against their black bark, offered a welcome sight in the late winter forest.

These hills rise as high as four hundred feet above the valley floors. Streams have eroded the thick cap of limestone bedrock, creating some of the most rugged landscapes in Missouri. Intense dissolving of the limestone underground over millions of years has sculpted deep caverns, some of which have collapsed into sinks. Underground streams in these caverns are the source of some of the largest springs in the United States. Some underground streams appear at the surface in closed valleys, and flow across them only to disappear below the surface again on the other side. Just south of Reynolds County is Big Spring, one of the largest springs in the world with an average daily flow of 276 million gallons.

*   *   *

Throughout the morning of Wednesday, March 18th, 1925, intermittent but light thundershowers dampened the rugged forest-clad hills of Reynolds County, sending local inhabitants scurrying for shelter. To them it was merely another reminder that spring had arrived in the Ozarks. But by mid-morning the wind had shifted abruptly from southeast to northwest, a signal to old-timers that cooler air might be returning; in truth, the unseasonably warm spell was about over. One hundred miles north, the St. Louis Weather Bureau duly recorded this wind shift.

Shortly before 1:00 P.M. storm clouds darkened the sky and soon became so heavy over the small town of Ellington that the lunch hour crowd, hurrying back to work, stepped up their paces. One among them, Ellington postmaster, W. F. Haywood, paused outside his office and carefully scanned the blue-black mass moving in over the western hills. He saw a jagged flash of lightning followed by an ear-shattering clap of thunder. The air became oppressive and deathly still, permeated by a sharp odor of ozone. As the blackness drew nearer, Haywood became more apprehensive, realizing that tornado conditions were upon them. He remembered the tornado of the previous September that had brushed the northern edge of town, unroofing two houses before continuing northeastward toward Annapolis.

His immediate concern was for the safety of his children and, instinctively, he hurried toward the schoolhouse. Moving fast, never taking his eyes off the approaching blackness, he had almost reached the school when, to his great relief, he saw the cloud, now partly obscured by a fog, moving east, skirting the town. For a moment he stood watching, his anxiety slowly ebbing away. Turning, he headed back to the post office.

*   *   *

From the rural mail carrier's report to Postmaster Haywood, we know that the Tri-State Tornado touched down north of Ellington. Its path continued northeastward, passing a half-mile south of the little town of Redford.

For its next ten miles across the deeply forested Ozark hills, there were no witnesses. Trees, not people, were downed along its track through thinly populated countryside, but fourteen minutes from its first sighting it tore through its first town, Annapolis, and almost simultaneously, through the lead-mining camp of Leadanna, two miles south of town. It is doubtful that the track of a single tornado measured two miles in width; most likely at this time two funnels moved on parallel tracks two miles apart, or possibly downbursts accompanying the tornado caused some of the parallel damage.

*   *   *

Downbursts

Downbursts are straight-line or fan-shaped bursts of wind that spread out from the point where a strong downdraft strikes the ground. They vary in width from a few yards to more than ten miles and can be caused by descending cold air often accelerated by downward moving raindrops. If less than two-and-one-half miles wide, they are *microbursts;* wider than that, they are *macrobursts.* Often downbursts are associated with tornadoes, and sometimes wind damage caused by them is mistakenly credited to a tornado, but the debris patterns left by the wind are straight rather than circular. Conditions that produce tornadoes also produce downbursts, but the tornado does not cause the downbursts—they can occur without tornadoes.

*   *   *

About 1:15 P.M., C. E. Pyrtle, a traveling businessman from St. Louis, strolled contentedly down the main street of Annapolis when he noticed the slate-gray sky had changed to a darker hue. Pyrtle, in town as a trade representative for the Penrod Walnut and Veneer Company of Kansas City, had completed his morning's business transactions, had eaten a satisfying lunch, and now prepared to leave town. Climbing into his automobile and closing the door, he glanced ahead and saw a huge black shape, traveling at tremendous speed, descend over the western hills, engulfing everything. Pyrtle leaped from his car and dashed toward a nearby store for safety.

He never knew what hit him. Five minutes later when he opened his eyes, he was lying on the ground, his head pounding. Raising his hand, he rubbed a large lump on his head. As he slowly rose to his feet he looked around in disbelief at a town demolished. He could see only three structures standing that he recognized from his previous visits—the school, a garage, and, eerily, a large old house now sitting starkly alone in the town's center, untouched. Unknown to Pyrtle, inside this house, in a dreamlike setting, a sick elderly woman lay abed, surrounded by a large gathering of family and friends. Although they must have heard the turmoil outside, apparently their concentration on the sick woman, most likely the matriarch of the family, totally absorbed their attention.

A torrent of rain poured down on Pyrtle who sought refuge in his miraculously undamaged automobile, where he waited out the second phase of the storm. Within fifteen minutes the rain stopped and the sun shone brightly, but Pyrtle, still dazed, sat inert, surveying the utter devastation surrounding him. He wondered if he were dreaming. Where shops and homes had stood he saw only piles of rubble, automobiles flipped upside-down, shattered glass everywhere, dangling utility wires, and trees lying across twisted lumber and plaster. Survivors now began to wander about, but they seemed to be in shock. Straight ahead, alongside the surviving house had been a restaurant, but now all Pyrtle saw was a huge pile of smoldering kindling. He watched thin gray wisps of smoke metamorphose into great puffs from which flames rose higher and higher, soon reaching the house, curling up in great orange licks all around its foundation.

Now Pyrtle reacted. Springing from the car shouting, "Fire!"[1] He raced toward the house, pounded on the door, and shouted so loudly that bystanders came running to join him. A woman opened the door. Upon realizing the peril, she pleaded for their help, explaining that the old woman upstairs could not move. Without hesitation, all the men rushed inside, bounding upstairs, and shouting for everyone to leave. Reassuring the sick woman, they gently lifted up her small bed and transported her down the stairs and out the front door to safety—and with no time to spare; the house went up in flames, a total loss.

After his dramatic act of rescue, C. E. Pyrtle drove to the nearby town of Ironton where he called St. Louis newspapers to relay a first-hand account of the disaster. As newspapermen there spread the story of the Annapolis tragedy, hospital personnel responded by gathering doctors, nurses, and medical supplies to send by rail to the stricken area.

This was an era of traveling salesmen: another in Annapolis that day had his own strange experience. At 1:15 P.M. he was eating a meal in one of the town's restaurants—possibly the same one at which Pyrtle had eaten not long before—and, because most Missourians ate at noon, he had the place all to himself. As he picked up his silver-ware, the tornado swooped into town, lifting the roof and all four walls off the foundation and carrying them away. Left behind, untouched, were tables, chairs—and the lone diner sitting in the open, still clutching his knife and fork, his food still before him. The restaurant staff also remained, shaken but unhurt.

Surprisingly, in Annapolis the tornado killed only four people, injuring twenty-five. At the time, many men were working in the lead mine at Leadanna, and older children were in the school building which, although damaged, protected all the children. The tornado leveled most structures, sparing only seven of the eighty-five houses. A retail merchant saved himself by diving under bolts of fabric just before the store fell in on him. Nearby, at the American Lead Mine at Leadanna, the tornado destroyed the tipple and hoisting machinery, forcing seventy-five men, working 465 feet underground, to climb through an air shaft to the surface. When they emerged the miners found hysteria in the mine settlement. Only thirty-three homes out of fifty-four remained standing and 90 percent of the mine property above ground was gone. Most homes in Leadanna survived because the full impact of the storm spared the town.

Mrs. John Thomas was in her house there when a hailstorm pounded it at 1:00 P.M. Fifteen minutes later while anxiously scanning the sky, she saw a funnel cloud advancing. In an instant she saw the barn sail off followed by the chickenhouse zooming past her window. It was all over in less than a minute. Her husband, working at the mill that afternoon, said he and his coworkers saw the twister descend on the settlement. They bolted for the cellar, leaped in, and barred the door, just as the mill collapsed on top of it.

*　　*　　*

The mine at Leadanna tapped the deeper lead deposits that once dominated the economy of the southern St. Francois Mountains in Iron and Madison counties. This is in the heart of the old Lead Belt, developed late in the eighteenth century by French settlers. The geology of the area led them to believe there might be rich mineral accumulations along the contact between what we know now as the Cambrian sediments and the old Pre-Cambrian granites. What the French hungered for in the Ozarks was silver. Inspired by the Spanish discovery of rich silver deposits in Mexico, the French hoped for equal success in Missouri, but, alas, they had to settle for lead, less precious but not without value.

In Missouri, French culture and language survived in the Ozarks and along the Mississippi River near St. Genevieve well into the 19th century. Even in 1925, French remained the language of choice in some isolated pockets in the mining districts.

Today, the lead mine at Leadanna no longer operates, and in fact the settlement is no longer there, not because of the Tri-State

Tornado damage, although it was significant, but because the industry found cheaper sources of lead in northern Iron and Reynolds counties.

*   *   *

Although the tornado lifted the train station at Annapolis off its foundation, the stationmaster within somehow managed to send a telegraph message for help. This, along with Pyrtle's call from nearby Ironton, reassured the townsfolk that a relief train would soon be on its way from St. Louis.

The logistics of preparing a relief train for a town suddenly struck by disaster is neither a simple procedure nor can it be carried out quickly. Organizing medical personnel, food, and supplies for temporary shelter is complicated and train schedules had to be altered. Although Annapolis was only 111 miles from St. Louis, the afternoon hours dragged on and no help arrived. Survivors began to fear abandonment, so much so that as nightfall drew near, desperation took hold, bordering on panic. When a relief train finally pulled in at 6:30 P.M. the mob of homeless people stormed it, many begging to be transported out.

A team from the Red Cross stepped down and took charge; in this case they were truly angels of mercy. Trained to quell panic, they set to work immediately, calming fears. Quickly and efficiently they set up canteens, kitchens, and sleeping tents with cots and bedding. Sizing up what remained of the town, they chose the schoolhouse as sleeping quarters for women and children, and soon they had all ablebodied survivors pitching in to help.

Fifteen doctors arrived from neighboring towns about the same time as truckloads of food began to pour in. Pullman cars provided shelter for the injured and additional sleeping space for women and children. By nightfall trains were transporting the seriously wounded to hospitals in Cape Girardeau, Poplar Bluff, and St. Louis. The less-seriously injured received immediate care in the town.

Finally, as calm settled in, the men of Annapolis built fires in the streets, using fallen timbers for fuel. These fires illuminated the utter ruin around them. Throughout the night, men huddled around these fires, quietly discussing their misfortunes. Just six months earlier another tornado had struck, unroofing or otherwise damaging forty houses, almost half the homes in town, and two years earlier a fire had destroyed the entire business district. The future of the town seemed hopeless to many of these demoralized men. Today, its population is only about four hundred, less than half that of 1925.

Continuing its race across the rugged Ozarks, the tornado entered eastern Iron County and Madison County, where the bald granite knobs of the St. Francois Mountains tower above the surrounding forest. Just south of the small village of Cornwall, at about 1:26 P.M., it crossed the tracks of the St. Louis, Iron Mountain, and Southern Railroad (SIMS). In about twenty-five minutes the tornado had traversed more than twenty-eight miles of Ozark country from its point of touchdown at an average forward speed greater than sixty-seven miles per hour.[2]

Leaving Madison County, still traveling northeastward, never slowing down, the Tri-State Tornado crossed into Bollinger County where it destroyed eight farms. Near Lixville, the Conrad School collapsed, injuring the teacher, Miss Oma Mayfield, sixteen of her pupils, and killing a ten-year-old, John Fulton.

It crossed into Perry County where it struck the community of Biehle at 2:00 P.M., killing four and severely injuring eleven. Now more thickly settled farming country lay ahead. At Garner School, near Biehle, the twister picked up and carried off the schoolhouse. Inside, the teacher, Miss Bedonia Bangert, and all twenty-five of her students found themselves in flight, finally dropped in various neighboring fields. Miraculously, all lived despite injuries. This incredible survival is listed among the odd happenings associated with the great tornado.

*   *   *

Biehle was one of a number of communities founded before the Civil War by Germans who settled south of St. Louis near the Mississippi River. Germans were the major immigrant group in the nineteenth century; many came as religious separatists seeking to escape repression. Political refugees fleeing oppressive reactionary governments in the various German states joined them. Highly successful as farmers, their settlements gradually expanded at the expense of their non-German neighbors. Becau*se they retained their German language, others perceived them as clannish and thus they alienated many of their English-speaking neighbors, who moved on. The census of 1870 shows that people of German birth or parentage made up 10 percent of the population of St. Genevieve, Perry, and Cape Girardeau counties. By 1925 almost half of the inhabitants of these counties named Germany as their heritage, and along with German populations in neighboring Illinois and Indiana, helped focus the attention of the German government on their plight after the tornado tragedy.

*   *   *

About a half-mile southwest of Biehle, the storm had separated into two funnels following parallel tracks. Two and a half miles northeast of the town it again consolidated into a single funnel and this time its intensity increased. It now swept toward the Mississippi River where it damaged some thirty farms lying contiguous to small settlements. In its last twenty miles through Missouri before reaching the river, about three miles north of the village of Wittenberg, the tornado killed four more people and injured another twenty-five.

Many people in these small Missouri communities lived in isolation, deep within the hills, miles from a railroad or main highway. To reach them, medical teams had to negotiate tortuous and muddy trails, fording streams, detouring around fallen trees, plodding through knee-deep mud. Early newspaper reports of what happened in these areas were vague and could not be confirmed because of downed telephone lines.

*   *   *

About twenty-five years ago I flew a small plane over the terrain of southeastern Missouri and southern Illinois, following the track taken by the Tri-State Tornado almost fifty years before. I could detect no signs of the tornado's passing, but beginning just north of Ellington, I set the course at 69 degrees, the same as that followed by the 1925 twister. As the Ozark country unrolled beneath me I gained a better perspective of the nature of the land over which the storm passed.

Clearly visible were the pattern of fields and fence rows that fol-

lowed the north-south and east-west boundaries laid out according to the United States Land Survey, natural guides to private pilots in the Midwest. But as I approached the Mississippi River it was almost as if I had flown into New England where land surveys predated those set out in the Ordinance of 1785. Below me the field patterns shifted— fences and roads ran in all directions. I had crossed into land that bore the imprint of the Spanish Land Grant boundaries, which were still being honored when the area passed to the United States in the Louisiana Purchase of 1803.

*   *   *

The violent forces of nature have a long history in southeast Missouri, as well as in other areas traversed by the Tri-State Tornado. From 1880 to 1925, records exist of at least ten tornadoes observed in the Missouri counties through which the storm of our story passed. In 1924, a tornado brushed Ellington and moved northeast to Annapolis, paralleling the path taken by the Tri-State the following March. Although this funnel remained above the treetops between the two towns, upon reaching Annapolis it dipped down and damaged homes there. Postmaster Haywood had good reason to be apprehensive about black clouds on March 18, 1925.

Leaving the state at about 2:23 P.M., our storm crossed the Mississippi River into Illinois. Just south of the crossing loomed a navigational landmark, Tower Rock, the *Grande Tour* of the French. This famous site impressed Missouri native son, Mark Twain, who described it in his *Life on the Mississippi*, as "a huge, squat pillar of rock which stands up out of the water on the Missouri side of the river—a piece of nature's fanciful handiwork and one of the most picturesque features of the scenery of that region."[3]

In it's passage through Missouri the Tri-State Tornado crossed relatively lightly populated Ozark country before reaching the more densely settled parts of Perry County. Even there it avoided all the small towns except Biehle. The toll of human life in Missouri was only thirteen; in Illinois it would be many times greater. The storm's most deadly forty minutes lay just ahead. In that brief time 541 would die. The Illinois killing spree was about to begin.

CHAPTER 4

THE CROSSOVER INTO ILLINOIS

NOW TRAVELING AT SIXTY MILES PER HOUR, the tornado came roaring over the Missouri bluffs, reached the Mississippi River and, momentarily, these two violent forces of nature crossed paths. The tornado's passage across the river took only two minutes—the river flowed on majestically, as it had for millennia.

St. Louis native and expatriate poet, T. S. Eliot, in his "Four Quartets," described the Mississippi River as *"a strong, brown God— sullen, untamed, and intractable."*[1] Here is the Reverend Timothy Flint, writing in 1826:

> The face of the Mississippi is always turbid; the current every-where sweeping and rapid; and it is full of singular boils, where the water, for a quarter of an acre, rises in a strong circular motion, and a kind of hissing noise, forming a convex mass of waters above the common level, which roll down and are incessantly renewed. The river seems always in wrath, tearing away the banks on one hand with gigantic fury with all their woods, to deposit the spoils in another place.[2]

At the point of the tornado's crossing, the Mississippi is a mile wide and like Rev. Flint's description, in many ways it parallels the destructive force of the tornado. This mighty river, 2,350 miles long, demonstrates the persistence of one of nature's forces, active for thousands of years.

*   *   *

At 2:23 the tornado came ashore on the Illinois side of the Mississippi, hitting the wide flood plain lying between the river and the Shawnee Hills; the forest-crowned bluffs of these hills are clearly visible seven miles to the east. Although they lay directly across the path of the storm, the bluffs did little to impede its passage.

The tornado struck its first Illinois house quickly. It belonged to Martin Meisner, a ferryboat pilot who transported passengers and vehicles across the river. Although he and his family were home they, and a neighboring farm family, were saved by the architecture of their respective houses—they were built around the original log cabins, a common practice in rural areas of southern Illinois. The log structures stood; everything else blew away. Three minutes after its crossing, the behemoth engulfed the little town of Gorham, and here not only did every building go down, thirty-seven of its five hundred citizens died.

All that morning of March 18 Judith Cox waited for a break in the weather, peering out from time to time, busying herself with household chores, hoping the heavy cloud cover and the frequent showers would lighten up so she could run errands and be home in time for her schoolchildren's noon meal. Her husband, like many men in Gorham, worked out of town on the Missouri Pacific Railroad.

As the rain became heavier and more frequent, her irritation at confinement changed into concern that her children would get soaked while coming home. They managed to time their walk home between showers and their safe arrival at noon and subsequent return to school during another lull in the weather left their mother still facing a boring, dreary afternoon. Around two o'clock, when the clouds again lifted, she seized her opportunity to visit friends working at nearby Wallace's restaurant.

Grabbing her raincoat, she walked the short distance down the graveled street noticing the oppressive and heavy air. In the strange silence she could hear her shoes loudly crunching on the rocks underfoot. At the restaurant, Lulu Mochenrose and Mary Clark greeted her warmly and as the three women settled down for a chat and a cup of afternoon coffee, the weather took an alarming turn. Rain began in earnest and hailstones as large as walnuts pounded the window. All chatter ceased as they stared out, watching the frozen chunks bounce about and pile up in the street. Suddenly it all stopped. As they turned their attention once again to conversation, the sky darkened so quickly that Judith jumped up, grabbed her coat, draped it over her head, and waved good-bye to her friends.

She later described her experience after opening the door to head back home: "I saw a great wall that seemed to be black smoke driving in front of it white billows that looked like steam." (This "steam" was water from the Mississippi River, driven forward by the twister.) "There was a great roar, like a train, but many, many times louder. 'My God!' I cried. 'It's a cyclone and its here'. The air was full of everything, boards, branches of trees, garments, pans, stoves, all churning around together. I saw whole sides of houses rolling along near the ground." She shut the door against the tumult outside but instantly she thought of her children at school and, irrationally, she decided to try to warn them.

"I opened the door again, bent my head down against the wind, and I started to rush out. Then the storm hit me. I was blown back into the restaurant and against the stove. The whole building seemed to shiver. It rocked back and forth. There was groaning and creaking and it began to fall. Fire was flashing in great puffs from the stove. I tried to get away from it. I was afraid I would be burned to death. But the wind blew me back against it. Then the walls fell in. The roof was falling. Something hit me on the head."[3]

She awakened in darkness, pinned down, unable to move. Instantly recalling what had happened, she realized she was buried under wreckage, but she heard the voice of Joe Mochenrose, the town butcher, calling out for his sister. Judith's muffled response brought him leaping into the wreckage where he began to lift up the timbers, uncovering at first a large red cow. It too was pinned down, its body holding up the heavier load; no doubt this red cow saved Judith's life. First Joe helped up the cow, which ran off bawling, then he freed Judith and together they searched for his sister. Nearby they found her lifeless body, a great gash in her head. In what had been the kitchen, they found the cook, Katie White, beyond help, horribly crushed. Mary Clark survived but with severe injuries.

Grateful that she could walk, Judith took off down the street toward the schoolhouse. The air was thick with dirt and dust; utility poles lay splintered with wires dangling alongside remains of demolished buildings. Ahead, through the murky atmosphere she spied her raincoat, which had been swept away when she opened the restaurant door. It now hung on a twisted pile of planking. As she hurried past she grabbed it and felt in the pocket where that morning she had placed her husband's paycheck. It was still there.

Complete chaos awaited her at the school. The large two-story building that accommodated all grades from elementary through high school had collapsed, burying the children. A crowd of rescuers dug frantically in the rubble. Students, bloody, many hysterical, wandered about, crying out for their parents. Judith Cox found her children, hurt, but alive, although almost unrecognizable. Their faces, like the others, were black and battered from grime and splinters driven in by the ferocious wind estimated to range in speed from 100 to 300 miles per hour.

*   *   *

Estimating Tornado Wind Speeds

Supertornadoes like the Tri-State have evoked many debates about the speed of the wind within a tornado. The incredible damage and strange tricks perpetrated by winds in even small tornadoes have led to some estimates that winds might exceed 400 mph and even reach 700 mph in some exceptionally violent vortices. Straws driven into trees, boards penetrating structural steel plates in bridges, heavy buses demolished and tossed many yards—such oddities inspire these unrealistic wind speed estimates. Until the late 1950s we had no reliable methods to measure such wind speed. Anemometers, previously used, fell apart when exposed to the full force of tornado winds.

Doppler radar made it possible not only to reconstruct the parent supercell thunderstorm, but also to measure the velocity of winds in a tornado from outside the vortex. Radar sends out radio waves and records the strength and frequency of waves that are reflected back to the antenna. These reflected waves are converted electronically into visual images on a screen. The brightness of these images indicates the intensity of precipitation, and the position on the screen tells where it is falling. Doppler radar further indicates the movement of this precipitation in response to the winds by measuring the "Doppler effect." In 1842, an Austrian scientist, Christian Doppler discovered that the frequency of sound—the pitch—increased if the source moved toward the observer and decreased when it moved away. We can note this effect when a train passes—as it approaches, the pitch of the whistle rises; after it passes, it falls. While serving in the Navy, I recall noting up-Doppler or down-Doppler—a rise or fall in pitch of the returning SONAR echo—to determine whether we were moving closer to or farther from a submerged submarine. This same principle also applies to radio waves, or to any form of electromagnetic radiation. By measuring the change in frequency between the outgoing radio waves and those reflected back to the antenna, the Doppler radar can determine, electronically, the velocity and direction of movement of raindrops, snowflakes, or other objects in a cloud.

Although the wind itself does not produce a radar echo, particles and objects moving within the rotating air inside the funnel do, and they furnish an estimate of the rotational velocity. But even these readings are subject to considerable limitations since the Doppler radar can "see" only the moving particles inside the tornado—raindrops, ice pellets, and debris. The National Weather Service now has Doppler radar stations around the country, and most television stations have them. They are designated NEXRAD stations—Next

Generation Weather Radars, rapidly replacing the Weather Service's old radar network.

Meteorologists first measured wind speed in a tornado vortex when they used Doppler radar to probe a funnel that struck El Dorado, Kansas on June 10, 1958. They obtained a reading of 206 mph. We know from recent observations that speed within a tornado can vary greatly, depending on its size and intensity, from 40 miles per hour in one that is weak (F0) to more than 260 miles per hour in an F5 vortex.[4]

Joshua Wurman, using a truck-mounted DOW (Doppler on wheels), observed the highest wind speed ever recorded when he obtained a reading of 318 mph (with a possible error plus or minus 9 mph) in the Moore, Oklahoma tornado of May 3, 1999. He took this reading from Doppler analysis of echoes emanating from several hundred feet above ground level at which tornado winds probably reach their maximum velocity. Prior to the Moore tornado, the highest wind speed ever recorded was 275 mph at Red Rock, Oklahoma. This reading exceeded the previous record of 231 mph, taken in a straight-line wind on Mount Washington, New Hampshire, 6,200 feet above sea level.[5]

*　　*　　*

A fourteen-year old girl, Alice Summer, who attended Gorham School, spoke from her hospital bed about her traumatic experience. When it suddenly grew pitch dark the students had rushed to the windows, but an alarmed teacher immediately ordered them back to their seats. "Then the wind struck the school. The walls seemed to fall. The floor at one end of the building gave way. We all slipped and slid. If it hadn't been for the seats (desks with attached seats were bolted to the floor), it would have been like sliding down a cellar door."[6] This girl, who was suffering from a probable fracture of the skull, burst into tears but continued: "I can't tell you what happened then. I can't describe it. I can't bear to think about it. Children all about me were cut and bleeding. They cried and screamed. It was something awful. I had to close my eyes. We tried to get out. Some did succeed in getting out from under the stuff piled over us. Then our fathers and mothers came and we got out." But at that terrible moment some fathers and mothers themselves lay buried under collapsed structures.

The hail and the darkness, which had so alarmed Judith Cox and the children at the school, also alarmed Earnest Swartz, the cashier of the First National Bank, not far from Wallace's restaurant. Alone at the time, like them he also hurried to the window to peer out. In amazement he watched the black cloud and the mass of foaming water come rolling down the street. But long before this, Earnest had made his plans for any emergency; in one quick movement, he grabbed the money and bank records and stepped into the vault. The door closed behind him just before the building collapsed. His quick action saved his life, the cash, and the bank records.

Wanda Mattingly, on the second floor of her large house when the storm got violent, had no vault to protect her and her children when she felt her home begin to rock. She grabbed her infant, Norman, and the hand of her three-year-old son, Charles, and started down the stairs. Halfway down, they saw the walls of the house fall outward and then the roof sailed off, while the full force of the wind struck them and swept Wanda's infant from her arms. She and the boy managed to cling to the banister, which held. Only that staircase remained standing. In a few minutes the storm passed and, to the religious believers (almost everyone) in the town a miracle then occurred. The Reverend Lee Brown suddenly appeared, Wanda's baby in his arms. The Reverend had crawled out from under wreckage and as he hurried to give aid to others, he heard the infant cry out from a pile of rubble. Thanks to the Reverend, the story had a happy ending.

Alice Temure, 70, a paralytic, lived on the outskirts of Gorham. She was lying in her bed when the weather became ominous. Sitting nearby, her husband and their son, Paul, both peered out the bedroom window past the great elm tree in the yard, commenting on the increasing darkness. From this window they had a panoramic view of a hill and, across from it, a cornfield.

Alice recalled her terror: "I could feel the tornado lift the house. It must have been raised ten feet from the ground and was whirled around the big elm tree. The branches stuck through the windows. Then there was a great splintering and cracking and one wall fell outward. I felt myself going through the air. I was stunned and when I came to I was lying in the cornfield across the hill. There is a little creek there and my feet were in the water. At my side was my husband. A great [railroad] spike had been driven through his lip. 'I'm dying Alice, dear,' he said to me. And we laid there and prayed together."[7]

Paul, who had managed to hold on inside the house, extracted himself from the wreckage, and set off in search of his parents. He found them across the hill where the storm had deposited them. Kneeling down, he carefully lifted his injured father and carried him back to the yard, leaning him against the elm tree. Then he returned for his mother and carried her back, but by the time he returned to his father's side he was dead.

Alpha Jones, a teacher at a rural school between Gorham and Grand Tower, outside the path of the tornado, lived as a boarder with the family of a student, Bernice Bright. On that Wednesday night, Alpha did not arrive home until 9:00 P.M., because after school she had hurried to Gorham to care for the wounded. She came through the doorway that night distraught and exhausted. Gorham was no more, she told the Brights. Many had died and the wounded needed medical care but had none because nearby Murphysboro, also devastated, had even greater need for help. The family sat up until late into the night discussing the day's tragic event. They decided to rise early the next morning to go offer help and take food and other necessities.

In Gorham, when they arrived in the morning, a team of nurses had already placed the seriously injured on trains bound for city hospitals. During the day doctors came in from Cairo and Cape Girardeau.

Volunteers directed the women to a nearby school that was serving as a temporary morgue. Once there, they headed for the basement, the center of activity, where bodies, laid out in rows, awaited washing. The shock of seeing the town in ruins had been difficult, but now the full human impact of the horror gripped them. For a moment they simply stared. Then the women quickly set to work helping to prepare the dead for burial.

From early morning to late evening they washed the corpses of men and women, adults, and children of all ages, blackened from wind-blown dirt and debris, many with grotesque wounds. These small-town people were used to caring for themselves and each other. For the most part hardy and stoic in the face of adversity, they prized physical labor as a manifestation of self-reliance. Washing the bodies of the dead was a service commonly offered by sympathetic neighbors. The townsfolk were close, many of them entering and departing this world near the small towns where they lived out their lives.

Bernice cooked and washed dishes all day in the school kitchen near the women, but afterward she suffered trauma from spending her day at the temporary morgue. Years later she remembered: "When I got home that night, I had one of the worst nightmares any little girl ever had. I was only eight or nine years old. In my dream, they dropped one of those bodies. It was Cheesie Krane, a good friend of my father. Both his legs were broken and turned and that was the vision that I saw."[8]

*   *   *

Northern and Southern Illinois

Geographically, climatically, economically, and culturally, northern and southern Illinois seem two different states. Illinois extends from the Great Lakes all the way south to the Kentucky border, and the boundary between "north" and "south" is approximately a line from East St. Louis, due east to the Indiana line. Chicago has the latitude of New England while Cairo, at the southern tip, that of southern Virginia.

In the humid continental climate of the north, winters are long and often bitter; summers lack the extreme heat and humidity of the south. Southern Illinois climate, by contrast, is humid subtropical with mild, rainy winters, and sizzling, humid summers. Tornadoes are frequent in both the northern and southern parts of the state, but early spring twisters are more common in the south.

In Illinois the tornado crossed the southern one-third of the state known as "Little Egypt," or, simply, "Egypt." Several stories purport to explain this name. In 1799 John Bagley, a Baptist missionary, traveled among the French settlements on the Illinois side of the river across from St. Louis. Coming upon the site of the broad expanse of the river floodplain from the high bluffs, he experienced a religious revelation, spread his arms wide, and exclaimed: "This is the Land of Goshen." He was referring to the biblical story of the pharaoh who offered rich lands near the Nile River to Joseph and his family. The Reverend Bagley also bestowed religious significance upon the prehistoric mounds at Cahokia, misled by their resemblance to Egyptian pyramids.

Reverend Bagley compared the Mississippi to the Nile, the longest river in the world, and he can be forgiven for believing the Mississippi its equal in length for, indeed, combined with its main tributary, the Missouri, it is the world's third longest behind the Amazon. There are major differences, however. The Nile flows northward through desert, whereas the Mississippi flows south through humid lands.

Some towns in the region bear Egyptian names—Karnak, Thebes, Dongola, and the largest, Cairo—but no one knows which came first, these names or the regional title, Egypt.

Still another legend centers on a series of climatic events in the early 1800s when short growing seasons befell northern crops, which failed, and farmers had to travel south for corn, oats, and wheat. The Bible was the Word, and many compared these treks to the seven years of famine in Israel that sent Joseph and his brothers to Egypt seeking grain.

*   *   *

After flattening Gorham, the tornado roared on across the rich Mississippi River bottomlands, leaving a trail of twisted and fallen trees and taking four more lives. It then traversed a ridge of sandy soils lying south of the village of Sand Ridge, and at 2:29 P.M. crossed the Big Muddy River near the mouth of Town Creek, ascended the bluffs near Abneyville Rock, and entered the wooded Shawnee Hill country. A special edition of the Murphysboro *Daily Independent*, published on the first anniversary of the storm, describes it: "The path of the storm from Gorham to Murphysboro to De Soto shows that the force of the winds were on the ground all the way, over hills and through valleys. At one point it passed through a ravine. It didn't lift and drop back to earth as the usual tornado does; it made a clean sweep all along the line, and was from three quarters of a mile to a mile wide."[9]

*   *   *

I recall more peaceful times along this flat plain. The bottoms were our favorite fall nut-gathering area. While still very young, I made many a fall trip in an open car down the unpaved Sand Ridge Road, winding through these hills southwest of Murphysboro. As we came out onto the bottoms, clouds of fine dust trailed our passage as far back as we could see. Ahead loomed the giant pecan trees, close relatives of the common hickory and walnut trees of the uplands, as they towered above the flat pastures. The trees lay just outside the tornado's track and escaped the fate of some of their neighbors only a short distance north.

My boyhood pals and I would wait until we drew near enough to see the brown carpet of pecans waiting under each tree before giving a whoop of joy and grabbing our sacks. Visions of fudge, thick with nuts, and nut-filled pralines danced in our heads. Hickory nuts and black walnuts satisfied, but pecans—they represented royalty.

Later, I often roamed those same Shawnee Hills along the valley of the Big Muddy River, obsessively searching for Indian relics. In almost every plowed field above the river existed evidence of a prehistoric settlement. Occasionally the disturbed soil around the remains of a tree, uprooted by the passage of the Tri-State Tornado more than a decade before, would expose flint chips, mussel shells, and potsherds from beneath the soil. None of these escaped my eagle eye and, joy of joys, more precious than a crown jewel, was a finely crafted arrowhead or polished stone ax. On rare occasions, my life became momentarily complete when I picked up a banner stone or pendant of polished stone, a relic of the Archaic period of five thousand years ago. It has been more than sixty-five years but I still occasionally find myself opening my box of treasures to admire their prehistoric handiwork.

Every time my path led over the crest of the bluffs on one of these numerous Saturday outings, I always stopped to gaze out on the broad floodplain, across the path where the tornado had passed years before. Parts of the woods had never recovered and the twisted trees testified to the power of that terrible event. In the distance, beyond Gorham, loomed Fountain Bluff, so tall that it hid the view of Grand Tower, just to the south, the site of another significant tornado that crossed the river from Missouri on March 27, 1890. This four-mile-long forest-crowned bluff cut off by the Mississippi from the Missouri Ozarks to the west, stands in stark isolation, three hundred feet above the flat plain that borders it on three sides.

*   *   *

Still traveling cross-country, racing sixty miles per hour, the tornado was now heading across these hills, straight for Murphysboro. My family and friends, along with all other citizens of the town, peacefully performed their daily tasks unaware they and their town were about to suffer the worst urban tornado disaster in the history of the United States.

CHAPTER 5

MURPHYSBORO

AT 2:30 ON THAT HISTORIC AFTERNOON my mother labored in the kitchen, completing her weekly ironing chore. She had set up her ironing board near the cooking range which, with its banked coals, heated the flatirons and kept water warm in the large attached tank. The southwestern horizon was visible from the kitchen window and looming above it were ominous clouds. Noticing the stillness of the air and the quiet, she paused in her work and scrutinized the sky; the strange atmosphere gave her some apprehension.

A sudden flash of lightning illuminated the semidarkness. As she put down her iron and hurried to the window, thunder crashed and, with a great roar, a fierce wind sent objects sailing past. An invading army of debris swept over the western hill—trees, boards, fences, roofs. Day became night. As the house began to shake on its foundation, Mother dashed into the connecting room where I played on the carpet and, without breaking stride, she scooped me up and propelled me into a northwest bedroom where she crouched over me in a corner. The house began to levitate and, at the same time, the piano shot across the room gouging the floor and carpet where I had played only moments before. The walls began to crack as the roof ripped free and disappeared, joining the swirling mass of debris. But the walls and the floor held and as we and the house took flight, my mother tightened her grip on me. We landed with a bone-shaking jolt.

Abruptly, all was still. We found ourselves balanced precariously on top of the remains of our garage, which nested on the remains of yet another demolished house. From a broken window we peered down from our lofty perch onto a tangled landscape, nearly unrecognizable. Instead of orderly rows of homes, we saw piles of lumber—here half a house teetered on its foundation, there an empty foundation gaped with no house at all. The once tidy street, littered with remnants of a town, lacked any coherence. Household possessions cluttered the landscape and everywhere trees left standing wore garlands of clothes, sheets, and articles of every imaginable sort.

Neighbors—some dazed, others excited—slowly crawled from beneath their wrecked homes, calling out to one another, comforting the injured. Other than minor bruises and scratches from being tossed about in our revolving house, Mother escaped injury. She quickly examined me and, discovering blood between my eyes, she extracted a protruding splinter of glass. With only this trifling wound, I too made the list of "the lucky ones."

A downpour followed, but it broke off quickly leaving a curious gray sky laden with dust. The ceiling of the room remained in place even though the roof was missing and kept us from being soaked. My mother carefully squeezed through a narrow gap in a broken wall of the house and, with me in tow, descended the heap of splintered structures. We joined the gathering throng, among them my grandmother into whose waiting arms my mother thrust me before she rushed off to find my father and my brother.

This story of our survival, told and retold to me by neighbors and relatives throughout my childhood, served me well as ballast for self-confidence and tranquility—I was cherished, my mother brave, but to this day I marvel at our good luck that the burning embers in our cook stove did not ignite the house and the surrounding wreckage, and that heavy flying objects spared us. Many others were not so fortunate.

*   *   *

The wall of blackness, accompanied by its noise described as "like a hundred freight trains," fell upon everyone too quickly for most townspeople to seek cover although some reported a wailing sound like a siren, as if the tornado wished to herald its own approach. At 2:34 P.M. most men were at their jobs, most women were home, and older children were in school. Recess bells had just summoned students back into their classrooms. Striking from the southwest, the mile-wide tornado smashed its way through the city, laying waste to 152 blocks and 1,200 buildings. Water mains burst and the pumping station went down; electric lines fell, wind-driven fires raged, and flames gutted fifteen additional city blocks outside the tornado's path.

During those first minutes of the storm, while my mother and I sailed off within the vortex, my father was peering out the door of his shop near Logan School. The schoolhouse and the hill on which it stood, blocked his view of the western sky and the shop windows faced east. Thus he could not see the colossus bearing down upon

55

him. He heard the great turmoil outside, and when he opened the door to investigate he spied his own automobile rolling down the street. Instinctively, he sprinted after it to secure the brake.

Inside the shop my brother's focus centered on his work. He had just crawled beneath an automobile when the building came crashing down. Protected by the vehicle, he survived without a scratch, easily crawled out, and sped off to search for our missing father. When he found him, unconscious, other survivors helped carry him to the hospital but because of his serious injury, doctors advised the family to transfer him to St. Louis. A few hours later a train conveyed him, along with other seriously injured victims, to Barnes Hospital there.

*   *   *

Murphysboro represented home to about twelve thousand people in 1925. To its south and west stretched the oak- and hickory-clad Shawnee Hills; a line of drab coal-mining towns extended north almost as far as St. Louis and east to Indiana. Nestled alongside, furnishing the town's water supply and much grief during flood time, flowed the Big Muddy River, a tributary of the Mississippi only twelve miles to the west.

Plagued by clay-hardened soils, few surrounding farms prospered, although apple and peach orchards flourished in the southern hills. In early spring their blossoms perfumed the air and offered a glorious sight for miles. During the peach harvest, among the hottest and most humid of the summer days, every person who could be recruited would pick, sort, defuzz, and pack the highly perishable fruit. I well remember the itch from sweat mixed with peach fuzz trickling down my body on those summer days.

*　　*　　*

My parents moved to Murphysboro during the decade leading up to the First World War. They grew up in the hill country to the south and married young. Upon arrival in town, my father took a job as hardware clerk, saved his money, and bought a grocery store. It gave him security and a good life for the family but he eventually sold the store, using the profits to open an automobile dealership and repair shop in partnership with my teenage brother, Granvil. With pioneer versatility, my father also had built a new house for us. As Murphysboro expanded into a bustling manufacturing and railroad center, it received attention in newspaper accounts for its rapid growth and vitality.

The citizens were primarily of Anglo-Saxon stock, augmented with a goodly number of African Americans and a mix of Germans, Italians, and Eastern Europeans.[1] During my newspaper delivery days, I came to know many of the immigrant families for the first time and to appreciate different cultures. On Saturday afternoons I collected for the week and I often received an invitation to warm myself at various potbelly stoves, to have a chair, and to listen to the Metropolitan Opera radio broadcast with my Italian hosts. I could go from one house to another, sit a while in each, and never miss an aria.

Although many were formerly hill residents, others had been coal miners who finally wearied of that brutal life. Most often it was the miner's wife who had instigated the move, having waited at the head of a mineshaft once too often to identify bodies brought up after an explosion, comforting stricken friends while silently grateful, this time not mine, thank God, not mine.

*　　*　　*

At Murpysboro Township High School, one of the first buildings in the storm's path, students heard the roar of the tornado's approach and watched as automobiles and trees flew past the windows. Their fast action—running to an inside wall—saved most of them. Corridors became virtual wind tunnels where flying glass and other objects killed two students. In the school's large assembly hall, 150 students were studying when they heard the wind; the teacher in charge ordered them down on the floor. When the hall's roof sailed off and its walls caved inward, most students leapt to their feet and, in panic, rushed for the doors; more than twenty suffered severe injuries in the resulting pileup.

Earlier, at Longfellow Grade School, Principal Joe Fischer observed his 450 students filing back into their classrooms after recess—so far, a quiet, routine day. But Fischer returned to his west window, preoccupied by the broad, black cloud in the distance. His concern turned to alarm as the darkness suddenly deepened. Bolting from his office, he ran from room to room ordering everyone to gather quickly in the downstairs hallway. As the teachers led the students single-file down the stairs, Fischer heard an awesome roar and realized that a tornado was already upon them. Raising his voice above the howling wind, he reassured the lines of children and their teachers. They remained quite calm, confident in his leadership, even though by now the building was beginning to shake. Consider his heartbreaking dilemma: The building seemed ready to collapse, but outside the tornado raged. He made his decision and instructed the ten teachers to lead everyone outside quickly.

About half were clear of the building when part of it came down with a terrible roar, crashing into the midst of the students remaining just inside the building by the door. Eleven students died under the falling debris. The walls of the school, weakened, continued to collapse even after the full force of the wind diminished. The main entrance through which the children escaped faced south and the wind had shifted to the north—the school was now on the retreating edge of the counterclockwise whirlpool of air and the remains of the building, miraculously, gave protection to those fortunate enough to be outside.[2]

Down the street, only one block east of Longfellow School lay the "shops," a railroad repair center and a sprawling complex of buildings. More than one thousand men worked there, Murphysboro's largest employer. At the heart of the center sat a roundhouse with a great turntable; here, workmen maneuvered the giant locomotives onto tracks that conducted them to numerous cavernous workshops waiting to store and repair the railroad's rolling stock. Thirty-five men died when these shops collapsed. One worker saved himself by crawling into the firebox of a parked locomotive.

As survivors there struggled from the wreckage, their first thoughts were of the schoolchildren, many of them their own sons and daughters. They made a dash for the school and leaped into the wreckage, literally tearing their hands to the bone in their efforts to free the children, and they did save many. In addition to the eleven who died there, many others suffered severe injuries.

* * *

Most school-age children sat in attendance when the tornado struck. The school authorities demanded good attendance and any unexplained absences received prompt investigation by the truant officer. Murphysboro's public education system was excellent—there were few frills, no bus trips (no school buses, for that matter), no politicians taking self-promotion tours through the classrooms (I don't remember many visitors at all), schoolchildren were not utilized as unpaid day laborers for community work, and one heard no controversy about religion in the schools. With more than twenty thriving religious denominations in town, the wall of separation was set in concrete. Practically every child who entered second grade knew how to read, since first-grade teachers devoted almost all their time helping students master this skill. Except for recess, lunch break, and the occasional fire drill, we studied all day.

*   *   *

Fires followed the tornado disaster and with the water system down there was no way to contain them. Many people who were trapped under collapsed buildings in the railroad shops and elsewhere perished in the subsequent conflagrations. One man survived for forty-eight hours pinned under rubble, only to die when the fires finally reached him. Firemen, hearing his screams, could only stand by helplessly.

Something of a miracle happened at Logan School two days later. Digging in the debris there, with little hope of finding more survivors, workmen searched for bodies. To their amazement they uncovered a dazed boy about twelve years old. He emerged not only alive, but uninjured. Air and sustenance brought him around, but he remains anonymous. He dashed off, crying for his family, before identifying himself.

Logan School, already slated for destruction and replacement on account of its substandard soft bricks, suffered worse storm damage than did Longfellow. Photographs show the building almost demolished. Some speculated that the lower death toll there (nine) could be attributed in part to those inferior bricks that easily disintegrated on impact.

Some surviving schoolchildren crawled from under the wreckage and, in shock, wandered home, only to find no house and, in some cases, no neighborhood. Years later a friend told me that upon reaching her home she had found only an open field; in the middle of it she saw her decapitated grandmother, still sitting in her rocking chair.

May Williams, a religious worker from the Who So Ever Will Mission of the greater St. Louis area, was in Murphysboro on that fateful Wednesday assisting at a revival meeting organized by the Reverend and Mrs. Parrott. Williams wrote to her mother:[3]

> We left the Logan Hotel about 2:25 P.M. and a goodly crowd was awaiting us in the Moose Hall. Mrs. Parrott opened the service singing *"More about Jesus."* She had sung the first verse and chorus, which we were repeating, when it suddenly grew dark and rocks began to break through the skylight. We were being showered with glass, stones, trash, bricks, and anything.

Panic reigned. The Methodist minister and Brother Parrott dived under the piano. May Williams and Sister Parrott, along with

the other worshipers with no place to hide, stood shielded only by
their faith. Williams wrote:

> We called on God to protect us all. Mother, I wasn't afraid to
> die. I saw the concrete wall at the back of the hall collapse
> and come crumbling in. Then the roof started to give way.
> From outside as well as from within, we could hear terrible
> cries, yells, screams, and there was a great popping noise.
> The wind roared—I cannot describe it—and it tore great
> handfuls from the roof above us. You could see shapes
> hurtling over us in the air. Suddenly from the bottom of one
> of the stoves which heated the hall came a great puff and
> flames burst out like tongues of fire. There was an explosion
> and the other stove broke. The whole place rocked. The only
> place in the building not damaged was the spot where we
> stood.
>
> Then the storm passed. We walked the city for an hour
> or more, terror-struck by what we saw. People went about
> almost without clothes, with no shoes on, wrapped in rugs
> or blankets. It was indescribable, the confusion. We picked
> our way among tangles of wires, trees, poles, brick and lum-
> ber to our rooms.

*   *   *

Accounts of storm damage and speculation as to the presence of
multi-vortices suggests that along part of its path the Tri-State storm
contained a number of suction vortices circulating around the tornado center (described by Ted Fujita in 1971). This idea is confirmed

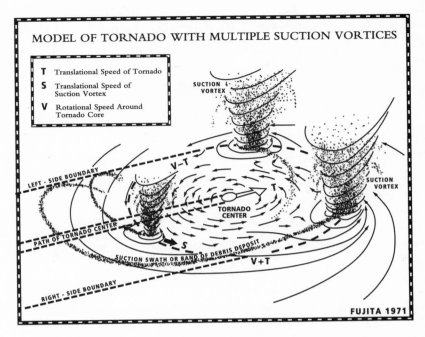

A tornado with multiple vortices as visualized by T. Fujita. Newspaper accounts of damage from the Tri-State Tornado in Murphysboro indicates it probably had multiple vortices at least at that point in its path. The rotational wind velocity (V) over the ground in the southeast sector of the tornado was increased by T, the speed at which the tornado advanced (V+T); in the northwest sector the rotational velocity over the ground was decreased by the forward motion (V-T).

by the following description of storm damage appearing in a commemorative edition of the Murphysboro *Daily Independent:* "In Murphysboro many eddies or swirls of the storm cut through the central and east sides, like scores of narrow tornadoes from fifteen to fifty yards, furious twisters, some of which demolished practically new cottages at Sixth and De Witt, wrecked the Christian church, Cross garage, power house and other buildings."[4]

Other eyewitness reports differed. "A number of citizens say the clouds were rolling over and over on the ground as it approached them from the southwest. Many didn't see a funnel shaped cloud, others did."[5] Some reported gray streaks marking the darker cloud as it moved on the ground and described it as steam. Others believed the streaks to be thin sheets of rain. Some pointed out that many of the buildings fell where they stood, as if a huge roller had crushed them. Most houses were found near their foundations, but a few, like my own house, were briefly airborne; some houses disintegrated completely while others remained intact; even after sailing off, some remained in livable condition. Workers at the brick plant about a mile north saw a large house and two smaller ones rise high in the air and disappear. The fair grounds on the north edge of Murphysboro were stripped of almost everything.

To the victims and to the devastated communities, the exact nature of the Tri-State was a moot point. Most observers were not knowledgeable about tornadoes and undoubtedly this accounts for the diverse descriptions of the nature of this one. Those who saw the storm clouds just prior to being struck by the full fury of it were, understandably, so traumatized by what followed that their descriptions can be described as confused at best.

Many expected to see a funnel when they realized that a tornado was upon them, and they may have imagined one. Most observers reported no funnel throughout much of the storm's path, and we must remain skeptical about funnel reports.

The belief that tornadoes occur when two clouds come together gained wide acceptance after this theory appeared in a popular 1887 book, *Tornadoes*, by John P. Finley. For years trained observers searched for verification of this phenomenon, but never found it. Again, we have a demonstration that people see what they expect to see—two clouds coming together and the inevitable funnel. Then there is the matter of a sulfur smell accompanying tornadoes. Lightning often produces ozone and its acrid smell might be assumed to be sulfur by some observers, and the smell of sulfur was commonly reported in tornadoes of the nineteenth century. Although ozone may be confused with sulfur, some observers associated it with the diabolical nature of these "agents of the Devil." People smelled what they expected to smell. Reconstruction of an event from the distant past is more difficult because of the influence of culture on perceptions.

*   *   *

About the time May Williams and her friends were arriving in Murphysboro from St. Louis, Michael Kiley sat at the throttle of a Mobile and Ohio passenger train enjoying his view of the early flowering trees on his familiar run north from Cairo, one of the most scenic sections of the line between Mobile and St. Louis. Passing through the Shawnee Hill country of southern Illinois, he made brief stops to take on and let off passengers.

As his locomotive crossed the bridge over the Big Muddy River a mile south of the Murphysboro depot, he began to slow the engine for this major stop before St. Louis. Kiley usually anticipated this last mile through the residential area south of the main business district. Alongside the tracks, separated only by a narrow street, appeared a line of houses where residents often waved to the engineers who sat leaning far out of their cab windows, watching for signals ahead. A warm camaraderie existed between those who lived along the tracks and the railroad personnel. Indeed, in this heyday of railroading engineers were well aware of their status and their responsibility as role models for small boys who dreamed of wearing the stripped coveralls and cap, sitting at the throttle of one of those magnificent engines.

But on that March day, Michael Kiley had other distractions. Ahead and to the west a dark mass of clouds rolled along the ground. A quarter-mile south of the station the wind increased and began to whistle through the cab and at the same time flying objects pelted the engine. He recalled: "We saw houses crumbling. The air was full of wreckage and the train was so bombarded by heavy planks that I was afraid they would pierce the engine boiler."[6]

The crew kept the train moving, plowing through wreckage that constantly threatened to block them. Train and tornado reached the center of town at the same time. Kiley stared in horror at bodies littering the street and buildings buckling under the force of the wind. A large grain elevator alongside the tracks suddenly collapsed and fell across their path, pinning them there.

After the storm passed, his path still blocked, Kiley sat in his cab and absorbed the desolation, "the most awful sight I have ever witnessed."[7] Rescue workers dragged survivors and the dead from the burning remains of buildings, others rushed by carrying the wounded and dead on stretchers, screams and shouts rent the air, half-clad people ran about panic-stricken. Walnut Street, the main artery through the central business district, was filled with demolished buildings and many of the structures still standing were on fire. Firemen frantically worked to extinguish the flames but they seemed to leap from every heap of rubbish.

Although Kiley witnessed many acts of heroism that afternoon, he singled out one person for special praise—an unnamed African-American cook at the Blue Front hotel across the tracks from the railroad station. Many of the hotel staff and guests had fled to the basement when the hotel began to sway, but when the building disintegrated they found themselves trapped and fire broke out immediately. Many burned to death. The brave cook, "cut and burned until he hardly looked like a human being," made trip after trip into the smoking ruins of the hotel to rescue the injured and carry out the dead. Almost three hours later Kiley saw him still working when the train got underway for St. Louis with its load of refugees and injured.

Medical workers labored through the night in a heroic effort to treat the wounded. They confronted many horrific situations as they toiled under primitive battlefield conditions; illumination came only from candles, lamps, and lanterns. In Murphysboro, of the 463 patients requiring surgery, large numbers suffered mangled arms and legs that required amputation. As anesthetics ran low, some surgery proceeded without pain relief, and by nightfall supplies of tetanus antitoxin ran out.

St. Andrews, the only hospital in town escaped serious damage and served as the principal treatment center. The Masonic Temple and the Elks Club in the center of town, and the damaged high school on the west side, also served as temporary hospitals. By midnight these were crowded with the severely injured, many barely alive. Both children and adults lay huddled, many with disfigured faces, broken and mangled limbs, and obvious mental trauma.

Dr. Joseph G. Bekirsch was one of the physicians who arrived from the St. Louis area and, like many medical professionals that night, he operated by the light of flickering kerosene lamps, trying to ease pain, ration the dwindling supply of anesthetics, and comfort those facing certain death. Finally resting after many hours of strenuous effort, Dr. Bekirsch stated that he had tended every kind of possible injury that night.

An anonymous Chicago physician became a local hero when a small girl with a broken leg arrived on a stretcher. With one look he realized she was suffering from far worse; quick tests confirmed pneumonia, no doubt from exposure to the elements. In the triage, when split-second decisions decided who was savable, she was placed among the dying. But her face haunted the doctor, and he kept returning to her bedside after long hours at the operating table. Applying all his skills as a physician, ignoring others' pleas that he rest, he labored throughout the night and following day, determined to save her. After thirty-six hours, the child opened her eyes and weakly asked for water. Only then, when her crisis was past, did the unknown physician rise from her bedside and steal away for sleep.

Many medical workers were volunteers who drove in from nearby communities to check on relatives, but then stayed to help. Lucille Howell, a teacher in a small town fifty miles to the east, loaded her automobile with friends and supplies and headed for Murphysboro.[8] Her cousin was a druggist there, and her first thought was to check on his welfare. She found him in near shock at the Elks Club. He had just helped administer morphine to an injured woman whose body had been pierced by a board driven through just below her breastbone. To remove it was impossible. They could only saw off enough of the board to make her more comfortable and ease her pain while she awaited death.

Workmen, digging in the rubble, encountered shocks even more ghastly than those endured by medical staffs—charred torsos without limbs, some pierced by planks and other wind-driven missiles, unattached arms and legs from victims of all ages. The skin of both the dead and the living, blackened from filth driven in by the wind, accentuated the horror.

A block away from the temporary hospitals, firefighters dynamited large buildings, sacrificing them to slow the progress of the fires that threatened to engulf the entire business district. Evangelist May Williams and her friends had found their hotel still standing although minus the third floor. They packed their things since the hotel had no water and no food. They planned to go to the home of a church friend but word came of her home in flames. By nightfall, as the fires came closer, they decided to head toward the station to board the next available train, no matter the destination.

As Williams opened the door, she and her companions stepped outside, descending into Hell. "Everything was ghastly," she wrote. "We had to pick our way to the station by the light of the flames. The air was filled with red-hot cinders and stifling smoke." Blackened, their eyes red, the stench of their clothes sickening, they trod streets blocked by piles of rubble, sheets of metal, shattered glass, downed utility poles. On nearly every block they met deranged people who wandered about, calling out the names of loved ones. She continued, "the roar of dynamite explosions added to the horror of the fires' glare. Truly we were refugees. The relief train came—dead and injured were put on first. We followed."

The train took them as far as Du Quoin, Illinois, where they found the hotels filled with other escapees. Even there they could not avoid the horror as more refugees kept arriving, many broken and in shock. One father drove in with his family, the body of his small son lay in the back seat.

Veterans of the First World War compared the damage inflicted by the Tri-State Tornado with the battle-scarred landscapes of

Belgium and France. In the flamboyant journalese of the day, a reporter describes the scene at Tower Grove Cemetery on the northwest edge of Murphysboro.

> A cold cheerless dawn even today cast warmthless rays over fresh mounds of earth and a score or more of crudely made crosses. A World War I veteran stood gazing over newly made crosses, out into the garbled horizon, tangled by the fiendish assault of nature gone amuck. "Four of those boys fought with me 'over there.' One of them is my brother. We saw Flanders together and he said to me: 'Bob, I'm glad we aren't buried in a mess like this.'"
>
> Bob's brother sleeps here amid surroundings that rival Flanders in all its battle strewn glory. Here ruin and death stretches as far as the eye can see. [9]

As during that war, casualty lists appeared daily on the front pages of newspapers, but unlike the usual lists of war dead, these included many names of women and children and in the town those lists numbered 234 dead and 623 seriously injured.

*   *   *

After my father became a hospital patient, my mother and I traveled by train to stay with relatives in Granite City, Illinois, across the river from St. Louis. Each day for weeks we climbed on a streetcar and took the long ride to Barnes Hospital to keep vigil over my father who remained comatose, his life hanging in the balance. In truth, my mother kept a death watch.

I had never seen a streetcar and the sparks from overhead were so fascinating to my young eyes that I remember to this very day the experience of watching them—perhaps my earliest memory. These marvelous cars so enthralled me that early one rainy day, with my very young cousins trailing behind (perhaps, being somewhat older, keeping track of me kept them going), I walked several blocks to find the flashing trolleys; the lights' reflections on the wet pavement augmented the magic. A two-year-old lost in a strange city: a further trauma for my poor mother. When she found me she wept with relief—but soon after, her life became complete again when my father opened his eyes and recognized us both. Eventually, we all returned home together.

*   *   *

While searching through old newspapers, I was startled to find my father's name on a death list sent by Barnes Hospital to a St. Louis newspaper, an indication of his close brush with death. It was my great fortune that he fully recovered and both he and my mother lived to old age.

*   *   *

Murphysboro lay in ruins, its citizens dead, dying, or in shock, its institutions destroyed or scarcely functioning. The tornado in its first hour and thirty-five minutes claimed the lives of 284 people and injured 856; already it set records for death and destruction that would place it among the great tornadoes of history, even though it was now less than halfway through its rampage. Ahead lay villages, coal-mining towns and farms across the rest of southern Illinois and into Indiana. The inhabitants were unaware of the horror approaching.

CHAPTER 6

De Soto

BUSINESS IS BRISK for former state senator F. M. Hewitt as, from his home base in Carbondale, he makes his rounds through the small surrounding communities. By midafternoon he finds himself in De Soto. There he wraps up the day's transactions with a stop at the home of a client where he lingers a while to praise and admire her six-week-old twins, proudly cradled in her arms.[1] As Hewitt stands facing the front window, he observes the sudden fading daylight and the unusual onset of early darkness—it is only 2:30 P.M.

As the darkness deepens he and the new mother walk out into the yard to investigate, she still carrying her twins. Across the street a neighbor, also carrying an infant, opens her door and steps out to scan the sky. She calls over to them, "Looks like a storm coming up," and they cross the street to join her. They stand in awe, perplexed by the strangeness of the atmosphere, so still and oppressive.

Murphysboro lies six miles southwest. Suddenly from that direction they see a broad churning gray-black mass racing toward them at tremendous speed. Flashes of lightning reveal timbers, trees, and flotsam of all kinds floating high in the air on the crest of the winds. To Hewitt, the sudden roar resounds "like a lumbering wagon coming down the street."[2] Shouting, "Tornado!" he gives voice to the fears of all. Now terrified, they turn and flee into the neighbor's home only moments before the house rises ten feet into the air. Amazingly, it gently glides to rest about twenty feet away.

Hewitt panics. As soon as the house lands, he flings open the door and bounds out into the still-raging storm. All around him in the semidarkness, houses and buildings rise, disintegrate, and melt before his eyes, all the while accompanied by that deafening roar. Hewitt finds himself caught up inside the vortex, lifted straight up, flying high. When the wind slams him down again, he lies stunned. Spying a post nearby and realizing it is his only anchor he crawls forward, his hands grasping mud and weeds. Finally he reaches the post and gripping it tightly, struggles to keep from being sucked up again. Later he is chagrined to recall how concerned he had been at that moment for his dignity—even in the face of impending death he felt foolish lying flat on the ground dressed for the business world, being flung about while grasping a fence post. If anyone recognized him, what would they think?

The ferocious gale subsides as abruptly as it began and all seems quiet. Although Hewitt's struggle to survive in the grip of the tornado lasts less than a minute, to him it seems much longer.[3] He continues to lie in the mud gripping the post after the wind ceases. When at last he releases it, he pulls himself upright and stands dazed, examining his body, surprised that he is not seriously hurt. Slowly he begins to walk around in a nightmare world. Corpses sprawl everywhere in unnatural positions—men, women, old and young—children, many unclothed. Then he hears the babies; their piercing cries seem to surround him, and only then is he aware of the women wildly dashing about, searching and calling out for their children. He knows he must help the frantic mothers, but no sooner does this idea take hold than he becomes aware of screams and moans from the injured, cries of "Help me!" "Save me!" "Mother!" "Here I am!"

He rushes from one casualty to another, each more desperate for help than the last. As he runs to and fro, unable to help any of them, the horror becomes insurmountable and Hewitt's mind becomes unhinged. Now completely overwhelmed, shock overtakes him. Desperately gasping for breath, suffocating, forgetting the women, he believes that only he survives in the whole world, and that he is dying alone, from lack of air. And then, to his great joy, a man comes walking toward him. He must be a phantom—but no—a real person!

Still in shock, Hewitt runs to greet this man, believing that the two of them are the only living people on earth. "I didn't want to lose sight of him," he remembered.[4] Perhaps the other survivor is riding on the same emotional roller coaster because he quickly agrees that they should stick together and they begin to pull the dead and injured from the wrecked homes. Working with this other person and concentrating on the task at hand, Hewitt's mental fog lifts and his emotional balance slowly returns. By the time rescuers pour into the stricken town, he begins to think clearly and remembers the women and their babies that he abandoned in the storm-tossed house. Guilt now overrides all his other tumultuous emotions, propelling him back to the scene where he finds all of them safe. They had remained in the damaged house throughout the storm, and its walls had protected them. They greet him warmly, relieved and amazed that he stands before them alive and unhurt. Rejoicing together, their friendship cemented in crisis, they, along with others congregated there, talk on and on, reliving their harrowing experience while comforting one another in wonderment and humility that they are alive amid the terrible carnage that surrounds them.[5]

*   *   *

De Soto, a small town of about nine hundred people, served principally as a residential town for families of men who mostly worked elsewhere—in the coal mines to the east, and in the larger towns of Carbondale and Murphysboro to the south and southwest. Thus, most men were away when the tornado swept through with its amazing forward speed, taking only two minutes to enter the town, destroy a large part of it, kill sixty-nine citizens, and depart.

It left behind a landscape so barren that archival photographs evoke images of nuclear obliteration. Not one building escaped damage. As in Murphysboro, fire followed in the wake of the demonic wind, and flames continued burning late into the evening hours, feeding on piles of lumber and debris. In some cases citizens lay trapped within these demolished buildings.

Mr. and Mrs. Frank Redd, who owned a general store downtown, died when they were trapped inside. In the smoldering wreckage of their establishment neither they nor a traveling salesman last seen there could be found. Later, at the behest of their families, searchers returned to the scene and this time they found the couple's charred remains; of the salesman they found not a trace.

A railroad telegraph operator, Max Burton, on hearing the news of De Soto's destruction, hurried to his automobile and drove toward the devastated town. Along the paved highway ("hard road" in local vernacular) from the north, storm-tossed wreckage blocked his way. He jumped out of his car and completed the remaining two miles on foot.

The closer he came to the center of town, the worse the wreckage, and when he reached his first destination, the school, he found the two-story building a mass of piled bricks. Only the lower sections of two walls remained standing. Twenty-five small bodies already lay on blankets with no one yet to claim them. The school principal hurried back and forth identifying bodies and helping search for more, even though he staggered and bled from his own injuries and narrow escape. He searched not only for students but for missing teachers as well. A large crowd struggled in a desperate digging effort, frantic as the ruins of the building smoldered. Firefighters from nearby towns worked with them, wielding shovels and picks, lending not only brawn but also desperately needed emergency organizational skills.

Burton decided he could best help by returning home to nearby Tamaroa to telegraph news of the disaster. Working his way back, he skirted piles of rubble, once homes and buildings; clothes and household items draped everything left standing. He saw such a huge pile of cars that at first he believed it to be the remains of a garage, but the streets overflowed in many places with wrecked cars. Dazed people, many partly clothed, fled the town in panic apparently just to escape the scene. Further along he happened upon two dead infants lying in a field near the city limits and two young girls on the highway, their faces bleeding, clothes torn. As he hurried past, he heard one ask the other, "How did you get out?" Her companion answered, "I climbed out the window. How did you get out?" "I don't know," replied the first.[6] The injured girls were pacing up and down the road in shock; they seemed to have no destination. In fact, many children were found wandering miles from town with no memory of how they escaped from the school building or how they managed to get so far from home.

The De Soto school building served grades one through twelve, and about two hundred students attended. Because of threatening weather that afternoon, teachers had shortened recess but no one sensed danger. When danger did become apparent no time remained to prepare an escape.

One student, Paul South, age sixteen, escaped serious injury by leaning against the south wall, which remained standing. He, like so many, described the noise of the tornado's approach as resembling many freight trains.[7] In the semidarkness, Paul could hear all around him the screams and cries of other children as bricks began to fall and bury them. He began to pray—"But I didn't pray out loud," he later emphasized.[8] He could see students raise their arms as if in supplication when the disintegrating building pulled them down. Rescuers found some bodies in that position. Thirty-three children died at the De Soto school—the highest tornado death toll in a school in the history of the United States.

After Paul crawled out he set out at a run for home, dodging piles of wrecked automobiles, bricks, and timbers all along the way. Finally reaching his street, the boy discovered houses in various stages of collapse, his own home a twisted mass of boards mixed with crushed furniture and other family possessions. Desperately he began to lift and cast them aside, calling out the names of the missing. Soaked with perspiration and exhausted he finally uncovered the broken and lifeless bodies of his mother and sister. But he had no time for tears—he could not find his grandmother. He began a methodical search of the premises toward the back of the yard where piles of wreckage lay helter-skelter. Underneath it all he found the seventy-six-year-old woman. His heart leaped with relief when she spoke. Dropping to his knees he grasped her hand to help her stand, but she fell back crying out in pain.

Paul never hesitated. Reassuring her of his return, he ran to the nearby highway, commandeered a Ford from its driver just entering the town, drove the car home, and backed it into the yard. With great care he lifted his grandmother and gently laid her on the back seat. Then he started out for the hospital at Carbondale, six miles away. (Fortunately, he did not head in the other direction, toward Murphysboro.)

Straight away Paul ran up against piles of broken timbers blocking the route. Undeterred, he maneuvered the car up onto railroad tracks paralleling the road, driving there until he could see a clear highway ahead. Within the hour, doctors were praising Paul for his fast action in saving the life of his grandmother.

Another boy at the school, Herschel Barnett, fourteen, survived and reacted in another way. In his schoolroom all was calm until the building began shaking. When bricks came crashing down Herschel crawled under his desk. Although injured, he squirmed out and set about helping dig out others. Back home his mother, Ida Barnett, had been caught outside carrying her baby daughter and although she made a run for the house, the twister overtook them, lifted them high into the air, and hurled them into the top of a nearby tree. Throughout its track the tornado lifted many people and impaled them on the branches of trees, but Ida, still gripping her wide-eyed baby, later climbed safely down. Of her three other daughters attending school, only one escaped by jumping from a first-floor window after a teacher screamed for everyone to try and save themselves; the other two girls died under the wreckage. Young Herschel helped recover his sisters' bodies.

Fourteen-year-old school friends, Margaret Neal and Beulah Millhouse, were sitting side-by-side when the bricks began raining down. They clasped hands and, with Beulah leading the way, dashed for the door. Margaret never made it. She lost her grip and immediately began to sink. Beulah had to continue her desperate run alone. Having to abandon others hopelessly trapped haunted many survivors later. Beulah retained a lasting memory of Margaret's terror: as she glanced back over her shoulder she saw her friend's stricken face just before it disappeared into the cascading bricks.

In the central business district, O. A. Ross, a salesman who had stopped at a butcher shop, saved not only his own life but also the lives of three others. When he saw the tornado approaching, he yelled for everyone to run for the walk-in icebox, leading the way only seconds before the building came down. Later all walked out, unscathed.

Two newlyweds standing on their porch had no time to run inside. They grabbed a small tree in the yard and managed to hold on although they were "tossed and beaten like rags in a gale."[9] They barely escaped death when a flying fender from an automobile whipped through the yard, struck the tree directly above their heads, and severed it as smoothly as an ax.

The family of Deputy Sheriff George Boland never found Boland's body. Observers last saw him helplessly caught up in the vortex some fifty feet in the air.

A few miles south of town a railroad section crew observed the approach of the storm and, hearing the roar, took shelter under a railroad embankment. Rushing to the town afterward and seeing the atmosphere of total chaos, each section hand headed for his own neighborhood with deep foreboding. John Bratcher found a pile of rubble where his home once stood, but no family remained. Only later did searchers find the bodies of his wife and twin babies some 150 yards from the house. The twins lay at least thirty yards from their mother, their skulls crushed.

Another section hand, John Cummings, discovered his family physically safe though traumatized. His wife and two-year-old had been entertaining visiting relatives when the tornado lifted them and their house into the maelstrom, whirling them around and around, and finally dropping the house several feet from its foundation intact, sans roof.

Mrs. Luther Stanley and her three-year-old daughter endured the worst of the De Soto carnage and escaped because of the unpredictable behavior of the wind. When she saw houses lofting past her window, she ran to the child, who slept on a feather bed and she gathered the coverlet around them both. When their house fell apart mother and child flew through the air, but they gently came down alongside a road still wrapped in their feather bed that had protected them from flying objects.

Fred Weaver, an Illinois Central Railroad conductor, was near the tracks north of town when he saw and heard the tornado. At the same time he saw a freight train approaching town. As he watched the storm a half-mile distant, he observed uprooted trees flying through the air. The train station rose straight up, sailed across the street, and smashed to bits as it landed. He saw the station agent standing outside the spot where it had been, looking skyward. A dedicated professional, Weaver realized that he had no time to spare;

he jumped from his car and made the fastest run of his life along the tracks, signaling the engineer who stopped the train just short of the strewn barriers.

Special trains were pulled in to help with the emergency, and on the highway, many drivers offered their cars as transport to hospitals. As news of the disaster spread, so many sightseers drove in that soon barricades had to be put up to block the roads and keep them out. As in all the stricken towns, the Red Cross, Salvation Army, and other beneficent institutions quickly arrived to set up temporary shelters and food kitchens.

Nearby towns absorbed the refugees that poured in. Their hospitals and morgues especially became overwhelmed. Carbondale, to the south, and Du Quoin, to the north, the first large towns on the main railroad and highway out of De Soto, received streams of humanity in need, followed the next day by family members in search of their missing. These towns became scenes of joy and celebration when searchers discovered loved ones alive in hospitals, but in many cases the morgues confirmed worst fears and scenes there aroused pity. Row after row of boxes filled with mutilated corpses lined these establishments. Queues of apprehensive seekers waiting their turn could hear shrieks and moans from within as family members identified their own.

John Bratcher found his wife's body in Du Quoin, but not his infant twins, and no one could tell him anything about them. He finally found them in a morgue in Carbondale. Such mix-ups occurred because volunteers—many from outside the community— participated in the search for bodies, and identities were hard to discern because of blackened bodies and distorted facial features from splinters, dirt, and severe injuries. One couple buried and mourned their young daughter only to discover her alive. Another family had found and sheltered her; after a time, the actual parents of the dead girl claimed her body.

*　　*　　*

Six miles northeast of De Soto, the small mining community of Bush became the next victim on the Tri-State's list. Scarcely a town at all, Bush housed miners and their families in rows of flimsy, almost identical homes. Seven people died there with thirty-seven injured.

Leaving Bush, the Tri-State traversed farmland for the next fourteen miles, killing twenty-four more and injuring eighteen in northern Williamson County and southern Franklin County. With its diabolic power and forward speed undiminished, it now raced toward West Frankfort, the largest city on its hellish journey.

CHAPTER 7

WEST FRANKFORT

I lacked many material things while growing up after the storm and during the Great Depression, but I enjoyed one priceless luxury in abundance—kinfolk, by the dozens: aunts and uncles, nephews, and cousins first-, second-, and even third-removed. They arrived and departed often, sharing their disappointments as well as their successes, and at times some needed sympathy and a temporary home. My parents greeted them all warmly, without judgment or favoritism, but I had favorites. One of them was my Uncle Bob, who lived on a farm near West Frankfort in the heart of coal-mining country. A miner by trade, he worked as a hoisting engineer for a large mine, New Orient No. 1. During eight-hour shifts, he operated machinery above ground that lifted the cages of men and coal to the top of the shaft, a coveted job awarded to him because of his seniority and because he had suffered a crippling injury from a mine cave-in. His good humor, intelligence, and easygoing charm appealed to me. I learned something about coal mining from him, the suffering of miners and their families, and the long struggle to improve their lives through organized effort.

We sometimes sat in his yard under shade trees and talked about most anything, except certain troubling subjects my parents advised me not to bring up. Nevertheless, one day my curiosity overcame their warnings and I said, "Uncle Bob, tell me about the tornado in West Frankfort."

A shadow crept over his face and he stared solemnly at the ground, deep in thought for such a long time that I keenly sensed my blunder. Still too young and too lacking in sophistication to apologize or change the subject, I only sat and endured the awkwardness until finally, in a low, sad voice, he answered, "I never talk about that." Then he returned to his silence.

I mumbled something about getting home before dark and I took off for the house to tell my aunt. As I departed by the back porch I heard my uncle call out, "Good-bye, Wallace, you come back soon." I turned and looked toward the elms as he lifted his arm in farewell, a gesture I gratefully returned, and I sang out my own good-bye.

As I retrieved my bicycle leaning against the porch I headed for the hard road and the eighteen-mile trip back to Murphysboro. I had the road almost to myself with only an occasional noisy flivver sounding its "ooga! ooga!" as it sputtered past. The flat countryside, level almost all the way through Bush and De Soto, offered easy peddling alongside familiar scenes of broad pastures, scattered wood lots, and cornfields as I returned home following the reverse route of the great tornado. Except for an occasional misshapen tree no physical evidence remained of the storm's damage, but from that terrible event some human wounds never healed.

*　　*　　*

West Frankfort, the most important mining and manufacturing center in southern Illinois in 1925, had a population then of about eighteen thousand. Its major employers within the city limits operated two of the largest underground coal mines in the United States: New Orient No. 2, the second largest in the world,[1] and Old Ben No. 8, barely a mile to the south and just beyond the reach of the great March storm. East of the city in the small mining settlement of Caldwell, another large mine, No. 18, furnished employment to many men who lived in West Frankfort. The city, while dominated by the coal economy, provided all the professional and business services of any city its size.

When the Tri-State Tornado struck, eight hundred miners labored underground at New Orient No. 2. Six hundred feet below the surface they stoically went about their grimy, backbreaking tasks, pickaxes pounding into the solid bituminous coal face. Pit cars on rails clattering to and from the hoists, sump pumps[2] thumping, air whooshing up the ventilator shafts, occasional explosions of charges set to loosen the coal—the mine resounded with a cacophony of nerve-racking noise. And always the drip of water from the layer of rock overhead collected in pools at the miners' feet before running off into the sumps, all part of a miner's daily life.

Explosions from a mixture of accumulated coal dust and methane gas claimed the lives of many miners throughout the years, but cave-ins presented the greatest danger in underground mines. The unusually high ceilings at New Orient loomed eight feet above the floor,[3] and though safety timbers lent support to these roofs, major cave-ins occurred. The sound of these supports cracking and splintering when a roof began to collapse served to warn the miners, giving them a few valuable seconds to run.

When employees in the mine office on the surface observed the approaching tornado at 3:00 P.M., they dashed into a large vault. (Most establishments paid workers in cash—the reason for large vaults at many work places.) Only one mineworker died at that damaged building when he failed to follow the others into the vault. He turned back to fetch his jacket and a flying object hit him.

The first inkling of trouble for miners underground came with a violent rush of air down the ventilating shaft that blew its doors open and collapsed its timbers. Such a blast of air indicated the possibility of an explosion in some part of the mine. Then the lights went out, machinery ground to a halt, and the hoist ceased to rise and descend in the main shaft. For a moment the darkness and the silence of a tomb froze the miners.

The bottom boss, taking no chances, organized an orderly escape. Miners lit the carbide (acetylene) lamps attached to their hats and hurriedly lined up in single file near the air shaft where zigzag escape ladders provided access to the surface and, one by one, all eight hundred climbed to the top. It took about sixty minutes.

Towering above ground, the mine tipple faced the full force of the wind. This tall wooden structure covered with sheet metal contained the hoisting mechanism and facilities for weighing, washing, and sorting the coal as the cage hoisted it, still loaded in the pit cars, up the main shaft. Lines connected there provided electricity for the mine. A separate structure over the air shaft housed large fans. These constantly sucked out stale air and removed accumulated gases while at the same time fresh air moved down the main shaft. New Orient's tipple, although twisted and damaged, remained standing.

At Caldwell, five hundred miners at Mine No. 18 faced a situation similar to that at New Orient No. 2. When their mine tipple completely collapsed, these men were laboring one and a half miles back from the entrance shaft 512 feet down near the bottom of the ventilating shaft. As wind whooshed down it reversed the draft and blew open the air shaft's entrance door. Bottom boss Robert McPhail explained; "This is a gaseous mine and the accumulation of gas was beginning to get serious, but everybody kept their heads."[4] They were fortunate to have McPhail in charge. Under his direction all five hundred climbed the steel ladder in the air shaft, the last man reaching the surface within forty minutes.

*   *   *

Few Illinois miners lived in company towns. The progressive state mining laws assured them the right to live where they chose, the same as any other citizen. Some commuted from other southern Illinois towns such as De Soto, Bush, and Parrish where once-profitable mines were played out.

In West Frankfort most miners did live near the mines but they owned their own modest houses. When the tornado struck, it bypassed the central business district and most residential areas. Crossing the northwest quarter of the town, it headed directly for New Orient Mine No. 2 and the row upon row of miners' homes constructed around it. The tornado reduced more than five hundred of those houses to kindling, not sparing the people within them.

Racing forward at more than sixty miles per hour, at any location the tornado completed its havoc in only a minute, and it required less than five minutes to cross the town. It came and went so quickly that many residents in the southern part of town did not even realize a tornado had struck. Once word spread, crowds rushed to the scene. Mangled bodies lay everywhere and frantic cries for help came from deep within piles of rubble. Hysterical survivors roamed helplessly.

The miners emerged into this nightmare world of "screaming women carrying maimed children."[5] They ran toward their wrecked homes and set to work digging out the dead and wounded. Since these neighborhoods had no paved streets a downpour that had followed the storm created an almost impassable mire; rescuers slipped and slid as they carried out the dead and wounded on improvised stretchers.

Throughout the evening shouts of jubilation could be heard as the more fortunate men discovered buried family members still alive. As one miner desperately labored in search of his infant daughter a fellow searcher spied a baby's shoe protruding from the rubble and, reaching to retrieve it, discovered a leg attached to the shoe. In one movement he extracted the infant, alive and miraculously uninjured.

Nearly all the delivery trucks and private cars in town served as ambulances. As darkness fell, the only light came from these rescue vehicles, flashlights, and lanterns. Within this emergency illumination, observers could see blackened miners still in their pit clothes running toward the makeshift ambulances, cradling tiny bodies. A reporter wrote: "Rescue work conducted by lantern in ankle-deep mud continued throughout the night. At least 2,000 people were homeless, and the townspeople opened their homes and hearts to them."[6]

*　　*　　*

We might well imagine the dilemma faced by the editor of the *St. Louis Post-Dispatch* on March 18 as he sat at his desk putting finishing touches on the late afternoon edition, with emphasis on the "Missouri" tornado. He had already sent a news crew to cover that story. By midafternoon he would have received word that the tornado responsible for the destruction in Missouri, instead of rising and dissipating, continued on, crossed the Mississippi, and at that very moment held southern Illinois in a state of terror. As editor, he would have recognized the amazing story developing. Now he needed another crew.

By 6:30 P.M. he had managed to assemble staff correspondents Richard Baumhoff, Samuel A. O'Neal, and a photographer.[7] They left St. Louis and drove the ninety-five miles over narrow hard roads and graveled stretches to Du Quoin, arriving there at 9:45 where Baumhoff then climbed aboard the first relief train bound for West Frankfort. Others in his group drove on to De Soto and Murphysboro.

As the relief train traveled south toward West Frankfort, passengers and train crew watched apprehensively as the sky glowed brightly from a distant fire. The crew believed the flames to be near Herrin, eight miles south of West Frankfort. Others suggested that West Frankfort might be suffering the same fiery fate as Murphysboro. Regardless of the fire's origin, it placed them all in a high state of anxiety. Their fears proved groundless—the flames came from a huge pile of smoldering mine waste in the town fanned by the ferocious tornado wind, but the "blaze kept alive the creepy awe of forces beyond man's power that the tornado first had instilled."[8]

*   *   *

Baumhoff reached West Frankfort at 11:15 aboard the first relief train to arrive, more than twelve hours after the twister struck. At the station two young men from the town emerged to greet Baumhoff and the arriving medics. He and some of the doctors piled into a waiting automobile—a "Ford of uncertain age"—and proceeded to the United Mine Workers' Hospital. They also visited other improvised clinics and two funeral establishments. Baumhoff reported that "the simple expedient of carrying a bag of first-aid equipment transformed a reporter into a doctor's assistant, to gain unquestioned entry."[9]

Although a complete medical team climbed down at West Frankfort prepared for work, they discovered local doctors coping so well there was no need for all of them, and some left to help out in nearby small towns. Local hospitals were filled, and churches, service organizations, and many homes had become improvised clinics. West Frankfort had turned chaos into order. Policemen patrolled and the dead lay in rows awaiting identification.

Baumhoff sent in this description of his first hours in the stricken city:

On the streets of the city, strangely silent crowds shifted about. Ambulances shot back and forth with noisy bells. The congestion of the wounded in their resting places, and activities of willing volunteers increased the confusion. Girls who probably never saw serious wounds before gave what help they could.

There was no outcry from the sufferers. Here and there

one moaned in agony. Faces above makeshift covers strove to repress the signs of pain and sorrow and fear. Men with fractured skulls lay quiet. Strangers comforted children with broken limbs. Maimed women sought news of their babies. Youths who could move a bit begged cigarettes. Those who needed major operations but had to wait their turn submitted gladly to opiates as physicians reached them. Everywhere the glare of electric lights and the stir of people kept the wounded awake.

Before midnight eighty-four of West Frankfort's dead had reached the morgues and embalmers were struggling against time in cramped rooms and interruptions by crowds of anxious survivors seeking relatives. Some of the dead lay naked, others only half concealed by sheets. Some bodies bore livid mutilations or burns. Formaldehyde fumes assailed the eyes. Worst sight of all, and one which turned everybody away with a gulp, was a row of sixteen dead children of tender years huddled on a table.[10]

Baumhoff hired a driver to guide him through the damaged area. Late at night, in a rattletrap car, they crept through mud in the most devastated part of town, finally becoming mired up to the hubs. Sliding around in the thick sticky gumbo, they were attempting to extricate the flivver when they found themselves surrounded by men who "appeared as from the earth," with shotguns raised. They turned out to be miners, some of them deputized, there to protect what was left of their meager possessions. They suspected the interlopers might be looters but after press identification reassured them they talked freely. One of them explained how his automobile had held up the walls of his house and saved the lives of his family. "His campfire was the one cheery spot in the vast area. All the while the melancholy croaking of frogs smote the ears. Barely discernible in the north was the bulky shadow of the New Orient mine tipple— stripped and twisted."[11]

Baumhoff had to travel to nearby towns to file his stories. But the railroad telegraph service was so overburdened that hours passed before his stories reached St. Louis.

So many sightseers poured into the town the next day that even reporters had to receive permission from posted guards to get in and out. By Friday some of the horror had begun to wear off. Grateful newsmen unanimously praised southern Illinois people for their kindness and hospitality. These mining towns had a reputation for toughness and journalists, expecting harshness, found nothing but cooperation and evidence of strength and character among the inhabitants in these worst of times.

*　　*　　*

Scientists have reconstructed the supercell thunderstorm that produced the Tri-State Tornado by combining maps from the United States Weather Bureau for March 18, 1925, and observations by eyewitnesses all along its path. From these sources they know that the supercell and its imbedded mesocyclone were unusually large— some thirty miles long from southeast to northwest, and twenty miles across; the average supercell measures less than ten miles long.[12]

In addition to these maps and human observations, a more con- crete bit of data comes from the office of Old Ben Mine No. 8. There,

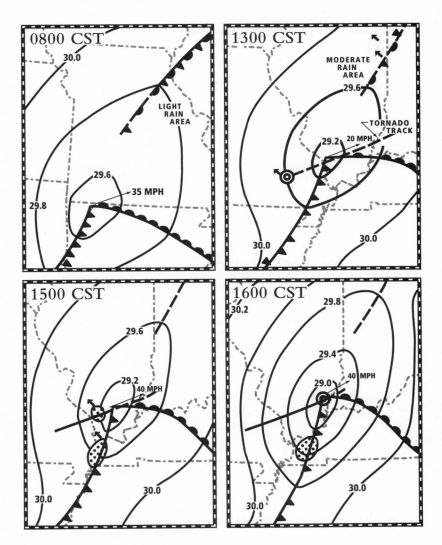

The surface weather map for March 18, 1925 with fronts added. The map for 1300 CST (1:00 PM Central Standard Time) shows the development of the supercell thunderstorm that spawned the Tri-State Tornado. The supercell and the tornado advanced eastward together, both reaching their maximum development as they crossed the Mississippi River into Illinois and maintaining their enhanced destructive power almost to the end. Another supercell developed south of the center along the cold front and appears in the 1500 CST and 1600 CST maps. This supercell may have produced some of the tornadoes that affected Tennessee and Kentucky later the same day. (Source: Wilson and Changnon, 1971).

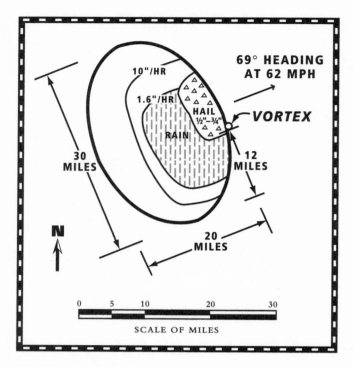

A model of the supercell thunderstorm that produced the Tri-State Tornado as reconstructed by Wilson and Changnon from Weather Bureau maps and local observations made during the storm. The position of the tornado vortex is at the leading edge of the cell just south of its center. The rainfall and hail areas are estimates based on local observations. (Source: Wilson and Changnon, 1971).

an operating barograph—an instrument for measuring and recording atmospheric pressure—recorded the passage of the Tri-State Tornado only one mile north of the mine. It produced a piece of paper just over three inches wide and twelve inches long that supplied the most precise meteorological data to come out of this great storm, and it confirms that at West Frankfort the center of the cyclonic system and the tornado arrived together. This fact is significant because meteorologists believe that the presence of the Tri-

State Tornado near the center of the cyclonic system throughout the twister's course contributed to its great power and long life. Most supercells and accompanying tornadoes develop much farther south from the cyclonic system's center—sometimes hundreds of miles— in the warm air ahead of the cold front.

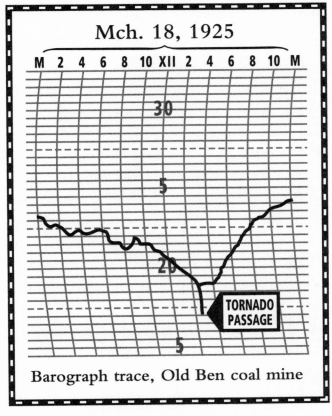

Barograph trace, Old Ben coal mine

A part of the barograph trace from Old Ben Mine in West Frankfort. The tornado's passage less than a mile north of the mine caused the barometer to drop suddenly; it then rose almost immediately again to its previous level. (From a copy of the original trace given to the author by Professor Lee Yoder in 1952. Dr. Yoder, in 1925 a graduate student at the University of Illinois, surveyed the Tri-State Tornado damage in southern Illinois for the U.S. Weather Bureau).

We can see from the barometer trace that as the cyclonic system approached from the west, the barometer fell steadily starting about 11:00 A.M. When the tornado within the cyclonic system passed just north of the mine at about 3:00 P.M., the pressure dropped abruptly from 28.9 inches to 28.7 inches; then it rose immediately, returning to its previous level where it remained for the next hour and a quarter. Afterward it rose for the next several hours as the storm center moved eastward.

The pressure reading on the barometer depended on actual atmospheric conditions—beyond human intervention—but the clockwork that turned the recording drum was set by humans and subject to human error. The clock on this barometer indicated the twister passed at 2:45 P.M.; all other evidence, mostly from stopped clocks in West Frankfort, indicated the time of the actual passage was 3:00 o'clock. The clock mechanism (set by humans) had been set wrong but close enough for operating the mine's ventilating mechanism (its purpose). Meteorologists accept the corrected time—3:00 P.M.—of the barometer trace, and it confirms that the storm center and the tornado advanced along the same path, but the twister moved at a faster forward speed, catching up with the center at West Frankfort.

Behind the cyclonic center during the first part of its course across Missouri, damage from the tornado registered mostly F3 and F4. Just before reaching the Mississippi River, however, the supercell and its tornado caught up with the center of the parent cyclonic system and, as it crossed into Illinois, the tornado increased in size and intensity. All across the state it continued to move faster than the cyclonic system—first a short distance behind the exact center, then catching up with it over West Frankfort, and finally running ahead of it to the Wabash River—but it remained relatively close to the low-pressure center of the cyclonic system all across Illinois. Only east of the Wabash did it move well ahead of the low center during its final half-hour.

Undoubtedly, its close juxtaposition to the center of the low-pressure system throughout its long run across Illinois contributed to its great destructive power. As previously indicated, its first forty minutes in Illinois were its most deadly, and its damage definitely reached the F5 category as it spread destruction throughout the towns of Gorham, Murphysboro, De Soto, Bush, West Frankfort, and beyond.

*　　*　　*

In less than five minutes, 148 people died in West Frankfort and 410 lay injured, but the tornado roared on through mining communities heading toward Parrish. Just over half of its long journey completed, already it left behind 554 dead and 1,426 injured.

CHAPTER 8

PARRISH AND EASTERN ILLINOIS

THE TICKING CLOCK high on the wall of the Parrish school indicated the approach of three o' clock as more than fifty children there prepared to head for home. Some of the more active boys had already collected their jackets and caps and were playfully slapping each other with them and laughing. But the schoolmaster, Delmar Perryman, no doubt weary from the long day, kept glancing out the window toward the western sky. Each time he did so, he became more and more uneasy. He locked the schoolhouse doors and, ignoring the students' groans and protests, he announced that a storm was coming up and all children were to remain seated and wait. From such decisive action emerge heroes. Within ten minutes the tornado smashed its way through the town of Parrish, leaving only three buildings standing: a church, a dwelling—and that schoolhouse.

Only a short distance away on Main Street, Clarence Lowman was also on alert because of the unusual weather. He stood watching from the porch of his general store when he saw the rapid approach of the twister and heard its mighty rumble. He ran to the open door and warned his business partner and father-in-law, James Clem, who was working inside the store; then he began a desperate dash for his home only two blocks away. He almost made it. As he crossed the railroad bed a few yards from his door the tornado overtook him. Unable to maintain his balance against the ferocious wind and feeling his body pulled upward, he desperately grabbed a rail. By now the noise of the wind had reached a deafening level and darkness descended. Sometime later rescuers found Lowman lying along the track, still clutching the rail, with a crushed shoulder, broken arm and ribs, and a possible spinal fracture. Ironically, the one dwelling spared in the town was Lowman's. Safely within, his wife, two children, and his sister survived unhurt. His general store lay demolished and James Clem, also with serious injuries, became another casualty.

*   *   *

Lightning and Thunder

Lightning accompanies all thunderstorms, and it is lightning that produces thunder. As cloud particles grow and collide they tend to acquire an electrical charge. A sudden flow of electrons between positively and negatively charged parts of a cloud, or between the cloud and the ground, creates this phenomenon.

These lightning bolts consist of a series of strokes with the average power of each stroke equaling millions of watts. We hear thunder when the atmosphere along the length of the lightning channel is heated to about 20,000 degrees C (almost three times the temperature of the sun's surface), producing a shock wave, compressing the surrounding air, and generating a sound—thunder.

Today, lightning presents a greater hazard than tornadoes. On average, eighty-nine people die each year from lightning, whereas an average of fifty-nine died each year from tornadoes throughout the 90s. Even minor thunderstorms that produce no violent weather may present a lightning hazard to people in open country. The safest place to be from lightning is in a building or automobile with the windows closed. If caught out in the open, crouch down to avoid becoming a lightning conductor to the ground, and do not seek shelter under trees.

*   *   *

Helen Brown and her eighteen-month-old son were visiting with her mother and sister-in-law. In midafternoon, while her child napped, Helen walked out into the yard to hang out the wash. An intense display of lightning followed by a crash of thunder so frightened her that she abandoned the wash and rushed back into the house. "Mom, I'm scared that lightning will kill me," she called out,[1] and hurried to check on her son. Just as she reached him, a large tree in the yard came crashing through the front of the living room. Helen grabbed her child and leaped behind the bedroom door. "The next thing I knew the door came down on top of us and then the whole house fell in," she related afterward.[2] After the storm passed, she crawled out with her son, unhurt; the other women, bruised, scratched, and terrified, emerged at the same time.

Then the hailstorm broke. Stones the size of lemons crashed down on the family. Spying a large galvanized washtub nearby that had blown from the laundry area onto a huge pile of furniture, Helen grabbed it and the women held it over their heads, shielding the child and themselves. The torrent of hail lasted but a few minutes and when it ceased, the three women searched for other people. Running from one demolished house to another they found their neighbors, some standing bleeding and dazed, some just in the process of crawling out from under twisted lumber. Moans and screams filled the air. Everything was flattened, the landscape scarred as if from a great battle.

*　　*　　*

Hailstorms and Tornadoes

The massive supercell thunderstorm that spawned the Tri-State Tornado and accompanied it on its long journey across three states also was an ideal weather machine for producing hail. Many observers reported hailstorms at Ledanna, Gorham, Murphysboro, West Frankfort, Parrish, and in Indiana, this hail sometimes heralding the approach of the tornado, sometimes following in its wake. The intense atmospheric instability in such supercell thunderstorms leads to rapid updrafts and downdrafts that favor hail formation.

Hail is the ultimate product of what meteorologists refer to as the Bergeron ice-crystal process, named after the Swedish meteorologist, Tor Bergeron, who first described it. The process depends on the physical character of condensed water droplets in clouds. Cloud droplets do not freeze at 0°C—they become supercooled. (Technically, 0°C is not the freezing temperature of water but rather the melting temperature of ice.) But if cloud droplets come into contact with solid condensation nuclei—particles that have the crystalline structure of ice—those cloud droplets will solidify into ice. Ice particles are ideal crystallization nuclei.

Cumulonimbus clouds—thunderheads—extend well above the

freezing levels in the atmosphere, even in summer. In that part of the cloud with temperatures between 100°C and 200°C, both water and ice particles can coexist. Most rain and sometimes hail falls from this middle layer. The lower level of a cumulonimbus cloud consists mostly of suspended water droplets and the upper cloud is entirely ice crystals.

Violent updrafts keep ice particles suspended above the -100å level where they continue to accumulate successive layers of ice from impact with supercooled cloud droplets, sometimes growing to the size of baseballs, more often to pea-size or marble-size layered spheres of ice. With the slacking of the supporting updraft or the onset of a down draft, the ice suddenly loses its support and falls en masse to the surface in intense hailstorms. Fortunately, most updrafts are only a few hundred feet across so that most hailstorms are of short duration and affect a small area.

*　　*　　*

A local Parrish farmer, Ed Karnes, had already survived a tornado in 1912 in Plumfield, Illinois. That one had destroyed his home. Something in the atmosphere that March afternoon in 1925 brought back frightful memories. On impulse he dispatched a farm hand to fetch his son from the school, about a mile away. He kept his eyes nervously glued to the menacing sky, and when he saw timbers sail past he realized his worst fear had become reality. He shouted to his wife that he was going to the school to rescue the boy himself (he could not foresee that the schoolmaster would save all the students). His wife intervened, restraining him until the storm passed. Immediately afterward they both ran toward the school. They found their son alongside the road; ironically, he was the rescuer, down on his knees bathing the face of the injured farmhand. He had found him lying there senseless, apparently injured by a flying object.

Dr. J. J. Partington, a physician from Cedar Rapids, Iowa, was on his way to Paducah, Kentucky that afternoon when, from two miles away, he saw the tornado envelope Parrish. He drove on to Thompsonville, commandeered all the surgical dressings and supplies available at a local drugstore, and prepared for what he realized would be a disaster. Meanwhile a train had pulled into Parrish and when the crew saw the terrible damage, they backed the train three miles to Thompsonville to seek help. It was perfect timing for the good doctor. He climbed aboard and, arriving in Parrish, organized a relief squad that helped place many injured aboard the train bound for hospitals in Benton.

The wife and children of the station agent and postmaster had been on the first arrival of the train, returning from a shopping trip in nearby Eldorado. They had departed from a vigorous little town but returned to find it gone. The postmaster lay crushed and burned near the train station lying amidst tangled wires of a fallen telegraph pole. He later died.

Many other horrific stories came out of this doomed town. A woman found dead in a field at least a quarter of a mile from her home could be identified only from her bright red hair. Her body was totally crushed. A family, searching near Parrish for their father, found his body in a clump of trees at least a quarter of a mile from his house, his legs and neck broken, his right arm missing, and with a severe wound in his head.

Everett Parks farmed a half-mile from Parrish. When he and his family were all blown a great distance from the house, Parks found himself clutching a fence post. As he glanced over his shoulder, he saw his young son flying toward him a few feet above the ground. He grasped the child by his leg, pulled him down, and held him securely, saving his life.

Later, a reporter who drove in from Logan over the winding muddy road toward Parrish found the first signs of the tornado about a half-mile out. He described the scene: "The road is lined with pieces of furniture, wagon wheels, clothing, bits of torn curtains and bedding, metal bedposts, dead fowls, trees, pieces of timber, and parts of wrecked houses."[3] A vast empty landscape remained where once family farms stood. The reporter saw horses and cattle, many standing confused among the many more that lay dead and maimed in the fields. The loss of farm animals in this prosperous farming country loomed large.

Horse-drawn wagons loaded with household goods and grim men and women crowded the roads, no doubt on their way to stay with friends or relatives, never to return to Parrish. Trucks filled with household furnishings and other salvaged material gave further evidence of this permanent exodus. Here and there people gathered in muddy fields searching for family, friends, or possessions. Clearing weather followed in the storm's wake; the reporter described the incongruous sight: "And over the scene of disaster, the wreckage and the anxious searching parties, a bright sun from among blue skies and white clouds smiled down."[4]

Parrish, a town of about three hundred, lay two miles southeast of the larger mining settlement of Logan (population 1,800), where most Parrish men worked in the Black Star Mine. The tornado passed one-half mile south of Logan while Parrish sat directly in its path. Most of the casualties were women and young preschool children. Before it fell, the town had forty-five structures. Besides homes, this included the church, a school, two stores, and a garage. Deaths in Parrish and in the immediate vicinity numbered twenty-two; with sixty injured. Unlike the other stricken towns, Parrish never recovered; soon all the survivors moved on.

In its remaining forty miles through Illinois the tornado ravaged prosperous farming areas in Hamilton and White counties, a section of Illinois sharing the rich Wabash lowlands with neighboring Indiana. It roared past but spared Hoodsville, Enfield, and the larger towns of McLeansboro and Carmi but farm casualties mounted and the toll was heavy—sixty-five dead and 140 injured.

In this farming area of southeastern Illinois, the tornado's northeastward course lay well north of the developed eastern extent of the southern Illinois coal fields. In Hamilton and White counties the land was gently rolling, almost all cultivated. This was prized farmland, the reason for numerous farmsteads that dotted the countryside.

A reporter, flying in a chartered plane along the path of the tornado on the day following the disaster, described its track across these fertile farmlands: "Houses [standing] are few and rare. Suddenly appears a vacant space, where it is apparent a house should be. There a barn with a few cows huddled near for warmth, and there a boxed hedge, lining what was once the entrance walk to a fine, solid American home. Down and down we go, to flatten out a scant hundred feet over a farm.

"There is the cellar. One can see the potatoes and other products still in their neat barreled rows, but there is not a semblance of a home, not even a scrap of torn timbering. And in front of this, an old man and a woman stand and gaze vacantly into the pit."[5] One can easily picture this old couple, gray and hopeless, no doubt in shock, contemplating all that remains of a lifetime of work. Trailing northeastward from the farmstead there is a long trail of debris—a piece of the house here, a timber there, "strewn like jackstraws for more than a mile."[6] This scene of farm destruction was repeated mile after mile in Illinois east of Parrish.

Just before reaching Indiana, the tornado skirted the southern edge of Crossville, four and a half miles west of the Wabash River. Howard E. Rawlinson, a schoolboy at Crossville Community High School, watched from his third-floor classroom window. Two of Rawlinson's cousins were working in the cellar of a nearby house, preparing sprouting potatoes for spring planting. It was a safe place for them to be but, unfortunately, when they heard all the noise above ground, one of them climbed the ladder and lifted the cellar door to investigate. He poked out his head just as the house shifted position and decapitated him.

Rawlinson related how he and his classmates joined neighbors later to help clean up the countryside, saving what was savable, burning what was not. They found many dead animals, one a Jersey cow with a two-by-four penetrating her body. They came upon a fence that had been ripped up and rolled into a large ball. Inside was a chicken, still alive but defeathered. They found the body of a woman impaled high in the crotch of a sycamore tree. Such horrors sobered and matured the schoolboys, Rawlinson recalled.[7]

The great tornado crossed the Wabash River and entered Indiana shortly before 4:00 P.M. It had now been on the ground traveling for three hours with its power undiminished. On the contrary its forward speed increased to an astounding seventy-three miles per hour at this point.

CHAPTER 9

INDIANA

Shortly before 4:00 p.m. the accelerating tornado crossed the silt-laden Wabash about twenty-five miles north of its junction with the Ohio River. Because of heavy March rains and melting snow the Wabash already neared flood stage. At its crossing point near the village of Griffin, the storm entered "The Pocket," the southwestern corner of the state where Indiana meets Illinois to the west and Kentucky to the south. With giant white-limbed sycamore trees lining its banks, the Wabash River long ago became a romantic symbol for the state of Indiana. It forms a boundary with Illinois along its lower two hundred miles.

In southwestern Indiana, the landscape resembled the rolling countryside of its neighbor, Illinois—cornfields, acres of wheat and oats, and the occasional pasture with its nearby wood lot. (Today soybeans largely replace oats and wheat.) From across the Ohio River the Southern culture of Kentucky greatly influenced this area.

A wealth of natural resources, particularly coal and fertile soil, combined with excellent means of transportation to produce a rich economy. Numerous mining centers sprang up in the late nineteenth century, with regional wealth giving rise to the important cities of Evansville, Vincennes, and Terre Haute.

*　　*　　*

Seventeen-year-old Orval Carter saw the churning funnels approach from the southwest as he stood in open country about a half-mile from its path. Two low hills lay to the east and west of Griffin, home to about four hundred people. The tornado moved forward over the western hill, and descended before a debris-laden cloud replaced Carter's view of the town. Timbers and parts of buildings rotated within a funnel that then ejected them, crushed and broken, across the intervening landscape. The adolescent stared fascinated, as the rapidly moving twister passed through the village quickly and departed over the eastern hill. Then he took off running toward the stricken town where a local crowd had already gathered; all were working frantically to extricate trapped victims.

Orval remembered: "Everything was strewn around, bodies, trees and houses." In the center of town sat the Kokomoor Restaurant, the one public eating place in the community. "From the remains of this building we heard screams and cries, 'Take us out!' We tried to reach them but the flames drove us back."[1] Seven people had gathered in the restaurant that afternoon for a late snack and coffee. When the building collapsed, those patrons escaped serious injury but could not climb out when the fallen timbers caught fire; it quickly engulfed them and all seven burned to death despite heroic efforts to save them. One of those working desperately attempting the failed rescue was the father of a nineteen-year-old boy trapped there.

Destruction of residential neighborhoods was particularly severe. Here in Murphysboro, the rather sharp boundary between the tornado's path of destruction and relatively unscathed dwellings is apparent. (Courtesy National Archives)

In De Soto, Illinois, one-third of the town was flattened. Of the 69 fatalities, 33 were school children, a record for tornado-caused school deaths. (Courtesy National Archives)

The Blue Front Hotel, near the M & O Depot in Murphysboro, was the scene of one of the major catastrophes of the Tri-State Tornado. Many guests and staff found themselves trapped in the basement and thirteen died in the fire that followed. Railroad engineer Kiley noted the heroism of an injured African-American cook who exerted superhuman efforts to extract the injured and dead from the hotel's wreckage.

The high school in Murphysboro was relatively new in 1925, when it was partially demolished by the Tri-State Tornado. In spite of the destruction, only two students died. In the
aftermath medical teams set up an emergency infirmary in the least damaged part of the
building. (Courtesy National Archives)

Logan school in Murphysboro was slated for rebuilding when it was almost completely demolished by the tornado. A new building replaced it and became the junior high school that I attended in the mid 1930s. Part of the building also housed an elementary school.

The remains of Longfellow School in Murphysboro. Here, eleven children died and many were injured when the building collapsed before they could exit. After the tornado, workers replaced the building on the site and preserved the architecture of the original. I attended this school from kindergarten through the sixth grade.

The school at De Soto, Illinois where 33 children died [final count although it does not agree with the 38 reported killed in the photo caption.] This toll is a record for tornado deaths in a single school in the United States.

Damaged house in the 1957 Murphysboro tornado.

A collapsed garage-possibly my father's-in Murphysboro, 1925.

Steps leading to nowhere. All that remains of a church in the southeast part of Murphysboro after the December 18 tornado of 1957.

A national guardsman hangs from timber imbedded in a tree by the force of the wind in the Tri-State Tornado. Logan School yard in Murphysboro, Illinois. (Courtesy Illinois State Museum)

Inset photo: The tremendous force of the wind in the Tri-State Tornado drove wooden timbers through trees and buildings. Two samples from Murphysboro are displayed in this exhibit at the Illinois State Museum. (Courtesy Illinois State Museum)

View of tornado-shattered homes on Illinois Avenue in Murphysboro, Illinois. March 18, 1925. [This is the street on which I lived when the tornado struck]

New construction was nearly complete at the First Baptist Church in Murphysboro when the tornado demolished it. People attending a funeral in the church basement escaped serious injuries.

Tornado destruction in a residential area of Murphysboro, Illinois, March 18, 1925. In the town of twelve thousand, 234 died and 623 suffered severe injuries. [Among the injured in my home town of Murphysboro was my father who was evacuated to Barnes Hospital in St. Louis, Missouri where he remained unconscious for several weeks]

Giant steam locomotives remained upright but were covered with debris from the tornado, which destroyed the M. & O. railroad repair shops at Murphysboro, Illinois. There are reports of one survivor who crawled into an engine firebox to escape the storm.

In the town, Mrs. William Price spied the tornado upon its approach. She rushed to her infant son's crib, too late; the wind swept the child out the door. Untouched herself, she ran out and found the two-month-old lifeless in a field. She herself then collapsed, and died, her child clasped in her arms.

George Westheiderman, a blacksmith on Main Street and chairman of the town council of Griffin, stood in front of his shop watching three funnel-shaped clouds approach and merge when they reached the edge of town. The speed of the advancing cloud astounded and overwhelmed him, striking him down before he could run. Afterward rescuers found him across the street from his shop, still unconscious, pinned to a tree by a one-half inch iron bolt which had passed through his lower right arm. He did not remember any blow before he lost consciousness.

Lucille Stallings, 12, shopping at Doll's general merchandise store, became buried when the building came down around her. She escaped uninjured but, tragically, she crawled out to discover her mother and father dead.

Although school had been dismissed at the usual time, 3:45 P.M., many rural children had not yet reached home. Their rural bus, a horse-drawn wagon, was on the road when the tornado approached and struck it down. All twenty-five screaming children spilled out. The driver and horse died instantly and many of the children lay injured, helpless in pouring rain. One heroic boy picked himself up and ran six miles to the town of New Harmony seeking help. A doctor there grabbed his medical bag and, with the boy as his guide, hurried to the scene. Others followed.

With open arms the citizens of New Harmony responded to the needs of the stricken Griffin people, filling their homes with refugees, opening up their schools, and supplying food and clothing. As scores of the injured began to arrive, the town turned their new school gymnasium into a hospital.

Not much remained of Griffin. None of its eighty or ninety structures stood undamaged with most houses and businesses completely destroyed. The school, churches, railroad depot, stores, grain elevator, homes, and one restaurant all became rubble. Five women and two men died in the restaurant fire, seven more died in the post office. Altogether twenty-five perished and 202 lay injured—sixty percent of the residents, the highest ratio of casualties to total population of any of the tornado-stricken towns.

One of the more fortunate residents of Griffin, Dr. C. F. Murphy, the only physician practicing in the village, escaped—a stroke of luck for the injured as he saved many lives before outside help arrived.

Intense rains accompanied and followed the tornado there, quenching fires and saving many people trapped in the rubble. Elsewhere rain-swollen ditches provided plenty of water for bucket brigades to douse most flames, although some had flared too quickly to be put out.

These heavy rains continued throughout the night and following day, causing another kind of emergency. The flooding Wabash River and smaller local tributaries inundated the nearby lowlands and soon isolated the town. The governor of the state arrived the next day and found himself nearly trapped; to depart he drove down a highway through a foot of water. Within three days, no one could get in or out of the stricken village except by train. The Illinois Central railroad, its embankment above flood level, became their lifeline to the outside world. John T. Noland of the Red Cross in charge of relief work in Griffin, reported that the submerged road to the north presented a serious obstacle, blocking movement of supplies into the village.[2]

When the tornado sped out of Griffin, still heading northeast, it struck the little settlement of East Forks, where it flattened most dwellings before heading for Owensville, thirteen miles from Griffin.

Again, as in Griffin, and in contrast to most reports along its path across Illinois, several funnel-shaped clouds moved in from the southwest. Whether they all converged or separated is unknown, but something hit Owensville with a great roar at about 4:11 P.M. It destroyed a church, but most damage lay north of town, with the greatest destruction in nearby rural areas where at least six people died and forty-seven required medical attention.

While driving near Owensville, Gene Goldsmith of St. Louis, a representative of the United Pictures Corporation, saw the twister sweeping across the countryside. He described a "dark cone, a shrill whistle, a mass of mud and debris."[3] The vortex missed him, but Goldsmith struggled to keep his car on the road. Most of Owensville escaped destruction but, as nearby farms fell, rural deaths and injuries multiplied. Three generations of one family perished when their farmhouse collapsed. Richard Waters, 70, his six-year-old grandson, two sons and their wives all died when that home blew apart.

The city library in Owensville became a temporary hospital, serving victims from the vicinity. Later, doctors moved the more seriously injured to hospitals in larger cities, the closest, Evansville, only twenty-five miles south.

Near Owensville the tornado shifted direction for the first time, and as if guided by some malevolent pilot headed straight for

Princeton, the third largest city in its path. Between Owensville and Princeton farms continued to go down. At the same great forward speed of seventy-three miles per hour, the tornado covered the ten miles between Owensville and Princeton in only a little more than seven minutes, striking the southwestern neighborhoods of Princeton at 4:18 P.M. It demolished the entire southern section of the city.

A reporter for the Princeton Clarion described the scene immediately afterward: "For a moment after its passing there was silence. The central and northern part of the city hardly guessed what had happened. Then began the ringing of telephone bells and presently cars began rushing up Main street, Hart street, Prince street, Gibson, Seminary and Race. Many of these cars were battered and broken; they bore a freight of dazed and bleeding human beings. They rushed to doctors' offices, they rushed to the hospital, steadily the stream of maimed—men, women and children—kept growing."[4]

Princeton's two largest industries were the Southern Railway shops and the H. T. Heinz catsup factory. Plant workers lived in rows of neat cottages near their job sites. Most of the town's forty-five deaths and 152 severe injuries occurred here.

Again, the catastrophe surprised everyone. When observers saw the looming dark clouds, they responded calmly, believing a spring thunderstorm loomed. When they finally realized the nature of the nightmare approaching, they barely had time to find shelter before boards, trees, automobiles, clothing, glass, sheet iron, all came flying at them. When this F5 tornado struck, it created a great terror; then it moved on in less than a minute. Stunned, the stricken residents crawled out, searched for missing family members, and tried to give aid to the fallen.

Luckily, the more than 500 school children from the Baldwin Heights School were home by 4:18 P.M. Bricks, steel girders, and heavy plaster fell across their empty desks and afterward the schoolrooms lay open to the sky.

The Southern Railway shops also sat empty, workers having left at 4:00 P.M.; later a twisted mass identified all that remained of the roundhouse, office buildings and the blacksmith and machine shops. Unlike the death toll at railroad shops in Murphysboro, only two people died at the shops in Princeton—a fireman and a janitor. Two more suffered injuries—a train conductor and the chief train dispatcher; both managed to crawl from the wreckage. There were reports in Princeton of loaded freight cars turned over by the wind.

At the Heinz plant, some employees worked the four o'clock shift when the multi-storied brick building fell. Only the lower walls remained standing. Surprisingly, only one person died there. Others in the adjoining greenhouse tending tomato plants escaped injury. There the terrible wind blew some women employees through an open door against a huge stack of tin cans awaiting filling and processing. The cans kept the collapsing roof from crushing the women.

Heinz superintendent F. F. Felts described the scene: "We had seventy-five persons, men and women, in the factory and about fifteen in the greenhouse. The force of the wind literally drove the employees into the [lower level of the] new building where they were in comparative safety. That prevented greater casualties. I and some of the others threw ourselves against a wall and escaped, though we saw timbers flying above us."[5] The tornado severely damaged the Heinz plant, destroying the roof, the upper floors and the engine room.

Although Felts escaped unharmed, not far from the plant his

wife and two sons suffered major injuries when their home caved in.

Alva Wilkinson and his wife had operated a neighborhood grocery store in south Princeton. He suffered severe burns, broken bones, and a broken spirit. His two children, Lloyd, nine, and Edna, ten, died when they attempted to run the short distance from the store to their home. In tears, his wife blamed herself for their deaths: "It's my fault," she cried from her hospital bed. "I told the children to run home from the grocery."[6] Although the children had reached home, before they could enter, the wind snatched them up and blew them down the street to their deaths.

To add to the Wilkinson's guilt and grief, their clerk, Riley Reeves, and the father, Alva, left the store to try to save the children while the storm still raged. Reeves perished and Wilkinson, in spite of severe injuries, crawled on his hands and knees until he retrieved the children's bodies and carried them back to the store.

The remarkable account of the experience of the wife and children of another citizen of Princeton, Thomas Deason, illustrates that some stories had happier endings. After the tornado passed, Deason had hurried home to find his car wrecked and almost nothing left of his house. But his worst fears proved groundless—he commented: "I am thankful my wife and my children are safe."[7] They all sought shelter against a wall but it blew down. A baby's highchair caught the wall and held its weight off them, saving their lives.

Neighbors who later examined the family's tiny refuge stated that it appeared almost impossible for anyone to have survived in such a small space. The local newspaper reported that "The angle between the fallen wall and the floor was so slight that only inches separated them from death or injury."[8]

In its less than three minutes of havoc in Princeton, the tornado killed forty-five residents and severely injured 152. This was the highest death toll of any single community in Indiana, accounting for sixty percent of all the deaths in the state, but only two percent of the 9,800 Princeton residents suffered casualties. In contrast, the twenty-five killed and 202 injured amounted to sixty percent of the people in little Griffin.

*   *   *

The Tri-State's Last Thirteen Minutes

Beyond Princeton this amazing tornado continued for an additional fifteen miles. Still one mile in width when departing Princeton, just beyond the city its width narrowed to one-half mile, but its wind velocity actually increased and its destructive power remained undiminished. Between Princeton and Oatsville it damaged twelve more farms. And a driver reported one more close call on the highway.

Businessman Fred Trenk of Indianapolis, drove toward Princeton late that Wednesday afternoon and somewhere along the way he picked up two hitchhikers. (In 1925 hitchhiking was extremely common and safe. Neighborliness extended to the highway.) As they approached the town from the northeast, they saw a "twisting cloud approaching at amazing speed."[9] Already it had crossed the city and Trenk and his passengers found themselves directly in its path. They leapt from the automobile and jumped into the ditch next to the road with perfect timing. To them, it seemed "just a puff and a whirl and then it was all over." Later they found the automobile against a road embankment, damaged but still serviceable. Strewn all around them were downed telephone poles and demolished barns.

Afterward Trenk, badly shaken, did not drive on into Princeton, but turned around and drove back home to Indianapolis.

*　　*　　*

Reports of detritus at locations some distance from its actual path on the ground attested to the monumental size of the supercell thunderstorm that must have accompanied the tornado all the way along its destructive course. At about 4:20 P.M. residents of Vincennes, forty miles north of Griffin, saw the sky become overcast as they heard thunder rumbling to the south. Suddenly, oak leaves, straw, cornhusks, pieces of shingles, weather boarding, and other remnants of buildings rained down on the town. This debris originated from wrecked towns and farms farther south. Looking upward, the residents saw swirling litter riding on the wind several hundred feet in the air. A half-hour later this litter was still falling on the city. By the time it all ended, trash covered yards, streets, and housetops in Vincennes. At the surface only a moderate breeze from the northeast kept blowing, but observers reported seeing high aloft evidence of strong winds and much turbulence in the rapidly scud-ding clouds. The timing of the fall of jetsam from the base of the supercell thunderstorm suggests that much of the initial fallout undoubtedly originated in eastern Illinois and in Griffin; that which fell later came from the vicinity of Owensville and Princeton.

Shortly before 5:00 P.M. a business traveler waiting on the station platform in Bicknell, about forty miles northeast of Princeton, saw a heavy object fall to the ground nearby. Upon inspection, it proved to be a sign bearing the name of a Princeton firm. The ejection of this sign less than forty minutes after the tornado picked it up in

Princeton attests to the high velocity of the winds aloft in the parent thunderstorm. To transport that sign from Princeton to Bicknell in forty minutes required a wind velocity of sixty miles per hour. This further supports the idea of the massive nature of the supercell thunderstorm that spawned the Tri-State Tornado and kept it alive for three and one-half hours.

*　　*　　*

In the open farming country of Pike County, near Oatsville, rural mailman, E. E. Williams, saw the tornado complete its fatal destructive run by unroofing a single house in Oatsville, then lift and dissipate. A Missouri rural mail carrier had observed its birth; now this rural Indiana mail carrier witnessed its last gasp, its great reservoir of energy spent. Thus ended its uninterrupted 219-mile track more than three hours after it began at 1:01 P.M. in the Missouri Ozarks, crossed southern Illinois, and finally lifted at 4:30 P.M. in southwestern Indiana.[10]

CHAPTER 10

The Aftermath

To the west of our house in Murphysboro, just beyond the neighborhood pond, rose a low hill overlaid with a thick grove of oak trees. Before March 18, 1925, this luxuriant area offered many open spaces for picnicking and recreation, but afterward neighbors found it a blasted tangle of gnarled and twisted trees. For many years this ruined woodland remained a symbol of the havoc inflicted by the great storm. Nevertheless, this destroyed park fed my imagination as an ideal enchanted "witches' forest" and I spent many carefree days there during my "Indian scout phase," building huge huts of grass from the dried up marsh that lay at the foot of the hill.

By the early 1930s those marshes were disappearing, drained as part of the WPA program for the purpose of controlling malaria, and a few surviving catfish desperately gasped for oxygen in shrinking mud holes. The frog serenade became more muted as ponds dried out. Following World War II the marshes disappeared entirely when dump-trucks deposited loads of earth into the swamp. For months, workmen labored to prepare the ground, to survey and lay out lots and streets, and to build houses. Finally my beloved playground was no more.

*　　*　　*

The nation and the world had reacted quickly to the great tornado disaster. Within hours, President Coolidge received messages from heads of state—from the Emperor of Japan, Benito Mussolini and King Victor Emmanuel III of Italy, the German government, and Great Britain, to name only a few. Italians and Germans were particularly concerned about the fate of their many emigrants residing in the stricken towns. Numerous recent arrivals from the British Isles lived in the coal-mining towns; many mine managers were Welshmen and Scots. Expatriates from Germany had continued adding to the population of the old established German communities and they had built a thriving brewing industry.

By coincidence, a great fire had destroyed parts of Tokyo on the same day the Tri-State Tornado struck. When the United States government offered Japan sympathy and aid, Yukio Ozaki, a liberal statesman and representative of that government responded:

> "The expressions of sympathy on the part of the American government has made a great impression upon us because it was entirely unexpected. Fortunately, the damage was not so serious as to necessitate aid from foreign countries. We feel deeply shocked at the news of the American disaster and extend our sympathy and condolences."[1]

From Annapolis, Missouri to Princeton, Indiana tent cities blossomed to shelter thousands of the homeless and railroads supplied Pullmans for sleeping. Temporary dining cars provided feeding stations for relief workers. The onset of colder weather following the tornado created an immediate need for such shelters. Many survivors lived in these tent communities for months until their houses could be rebuilt and, like refugee groups everywhere, they offered consolation and support to one another.

Although many citizens of the smaller towns which had been all but wiped out—Annapolis, Gorham, De Soto, Parrish, and Griffin—expressed doubts that their towns would ever recover, most people vowed to rebuild. The tenor of the times was positive. After all in the roaring twenties the nation enjoyed unprecedented prosperity; with a stock market rising every day, money for rebuilding presented no problem.

One year later the Murphysboro *Daily Independent* published a commemorative issue retelling many events of the storm. It featured not only stories about the remarkable recovery of the town but also of the entire region. In the issue the editors expressed gratitude to all who had rushed to help.

Miles of dirt and gravel roads had been transformed into paved highways—the hard roads—in the aftermath of World War I. Although highways had not yet replaced railroads as the primary routes of transport and travel, a network of these roads gave an alternative access to most of the stricken communities. Afterward, these paved roads had furnished a supplemental means of transporting the injured to hospitals.

Money poured in for rehabilitation, and relief collection agencies sprang up in major cities. The *St. Louis Post-Dispatch* initiated a drive for donations, and the *Chicago Tribune* did the same. The Red Cross and Salvation Army organized special collections. Lists of contributors appeared daily on the front pages of newspapers. Other groups, secular and religious, joined these well-known charities.

Teams from various national relief organizations arrived immediately, equipped to serve. Along with the National Guard relief workers not only helped set up temporary shelter but they also supplied nurses and other medical personnel to assist exhausted local health professionals.

For years a controversy raged over fairness in the distribution of funds. Critics were plentiful, as were citizens who defended the selection process. Insurance companies received their share of criticism. Some claimed that because fire destroyed their property, insurance companies refused to pay because their tornado policies did not specifically mention fire damage. Others whose homes fell from the storm ferocity first and then burned, received no insurance payment because their policy covered only fire loss, but did not mention storm damage. The Red Cross received the brunt of citizens' anger. Many believed that the rich received total compensation for their losses, the "hard-working" middle class received only a small measure, and the "shiftless" poor were handed more than they deserved.

Local newspaper editors took a more benign view of relief aid as expressed in the following editorial comment:

> From all over the country we hear that there is a spontaneous offering of help. This will be sent to people who are not in a position to help themselves, but the committees must not depend on the requests for help. Many of the most deserving will suffer and starve before they overcome their pride and ask for aid. Search for this kind of people—they are deserving.
>
> Another class who must not be forgotten are those in the rural districts. Because they are away from the city centers they may be overlooked.[2]

In Murphysboro local plans to begin reconstruction through organization of citizens began immediately. Residents gave much credit to attorney Isaac Levy, who provided the leadership. When the tornado struck, Levy was conducting a court case in Jonesboro, a small town about twenty miles south of Murphysboro. He rushed home to find his new house severely damaged but his wife and infant daughter were not injured. He immediately offered his services to other community leaders to coordinate the many tasks that lay ahead. In an appeal to the nation, he made the following statement as general chairman of the relief committee:

> The nation at large cannot fully realize or appreciate the great loss and damage that the people of Murphysboro and vicinity have sustained as a result of the terrible storm of last Wednesday, and of the fire which followed; the consequences are staggering. The loss of life is great and the number of people suffering from personal injuries is enormous. The loss of property is stupendous and is so great and complete that a personal visit to the stricken area is necessary to comprehend our present predicament.[3]

Levy also provided the optimism about Murphysboro's ability to rise again as a prosperous city. After meeting with the major businessmen of the town, he had this to say about its long-term prospects:

> We shall see a new Murphysboro—a new building and a new home and contents for those destroyed. Our industries are not to penalize Murphysboro just because of her misfortunes. Leaders from the Mobile & Ohio Railroad came to me in person with the assurance the company will do all in its

power here. They offered transportation anywhere on their line for the living or the dead. I feel sure the M & O [Mobile and Ohio] is not going to add to Murphysboro's suffering by refusing to rebuild. [4]

Mr. Levy's faith in the M & O railroad proved misplaced. The company never rebuilt the repair shops but moved them to Jackson, Mississippi. I remember the vast, weed-infested open spaces where the former repair shops once stood. In the 1930s numerous footpaths crisscrossed the area, furnishing shortcuts from my part of town to the junior high school and to the central business district. During that time, I often noted numerous scavengers excavating the piles of rusting metal to sell to scrap dealers.

The Brown Shoe Company's plant was much less damaged than the shops and this company did rebuild in their same location. The shoe factory remained a vital workplace well into the post-World War II era. Citizens could set their clocks by the factory whistle. During my newspaper delivery years, I relied on that 7:00 A.M. whistle. If I had not completed my route by then, I rushed to do so. We all assumed that most of our classmates would go to work at the factory—jokingly we referred to it as "Brown's College."

*   *   *

A team of structural engineers who surveyed the scene of the destruction in the summer of 1925 produced a long report suggesting changes in design of buildings and bridges to better withstand tornadoes.[5] The committee also considered the factors that made the deaths and injuries so high and these are summarized here:

(1) *Lack of any tornado forecast*

(2) *Lack of immediate warning that a massive tornado moved in their direction*   An advanced warning of thirty minutes to one hour would have permitted many to seek shelter and the death toll would not have been so high.

(3) *Exceptionally high speed of forward movement*   The speed at which the tornado advanced not only caught many victims unaware but also added to the force of the wind within the vortex. The forward speed of the tornado increased the velocity of the wind in the southeast quadrant of the storm—a rotational speed of 200 mph became 260 mph when the 60 mph forward motion of the vortex was added, but the advancing speed would effectively reduce the rotation velocity in reference to the ground to 140 mph on the northwestern part of the storm.

(4) *Unusually large storm*   The long track and wide path spread the damage over 164 square miles compared to about three and one-half square miles of damage produced by the average tornado. This fact alone accounts for the extreme damage wrought by the storm. Overall the Tri-State Tornado caused four deaths per square mile, but if we consider only built-up areas, it is much higher. In Murphysboro, for example, deaths were more than 100 per square mile in the two-and-a-half-square miles of destruction. By comparison, in the Galveston hurricane of 1900, deaths within the city set records for loss of life from a windstorm, but deaths per square mile were little more than those suffered in Murphysboro.

(5) *Lack of adequate shelter*   Many homes in the storm's path had no storm shelters or basements, and persons who sought shelter by lying in shallow depressions often met death or injury from flying objects or falling debris. As the tornado moved eastward its load of missiles increased.

(6) *Lack of tornado appearance*   A visual sighting of a twister would have given three to five minutes warning before it struck. Although persons in the storm's path heard the loud roar and whine one or two minutes before it arrived, it often failed to alert them to seek what shelter was available.

(7) *Poor construction techniques*   Many of the destroyed residences were poorly constructed frame houses not adequately anchored to their foundations. Construction for many commercial and industrial buildings as well failed to meet minimal building criteria.

*   *   *

Workmen were able somehow to lift our home from the piles of lumber intact. One of my earliest memories was standing and watching those men move it. One burly worker, seeing me nearby, walked over and, taking my hand, escorted me to the work site and placed my hand on the turning bar of the large jack they were using to raise the house. Instructing me to push the handle (he surreptitiously pulled on the other end), I went through the motions of helping put my house back on its foundation. I can still see the crew smiling and congratulating me on what a good job I did helping them.

For many older survivors, sadness became a daily reality. In our neighborhood lived a couple whose only child died when Logan School collapsed. While still small I began to visit the Roberts and to feed and talk to their large green and red parrot. Every time I knocked on their door they greeted me with great affection and out would come their box of keepsakes—small toys, books, a bag of marbles—once the possessions of their son. Along with cookies and milk, they fed me stories of Paul's too-short life and I quietly listened while I stared at his framed, enlarged photograph on the table. Their stories became as familiar to me as were the folktales my grandmother enjoyed telling. The Roberts lived somewhat isolated, a quiet couple. After I matured, even in my twenties, I continued to visit them occasionally and they always greeted me the same way (Yes, the parrot was still there). I came to realize that, in a small way, I had substituted for their lost son. They had watched me grow up. Such permanent mourning shadowed many homes in Murphysboro. For the Roberts and other grieving families, the tornado came and stayed.

*　　*　　*

The stock market crash of 1929 brought the four years of reconstruction from the Tri-State Tornado to an abrupt halt. The area never fully recovered. Even today, most of the stricken towns have fewer people. West Frankfort has less than half the population it had in 1925. With the exception of Murphysboro and Carbondale in Jackson County, where Southern Illinois University stimulates economic growth, Little Egypt has the highest unemployment rate in Illinois. It was not until after World War II, when the boys came home and new young families provided economic stimulus and a building boom, that all the tornado scars finally disappeared.

In any case, even the final four years of prosperity after the tornado were unkind to the coal miners. Decline had already begun in the coal fields—1925 happened to be the peak year for coal production from the underground mines in Williamson and Franklin counties. After that, it was a slow, ever-deepening recession in the mines that accelerated during the depression years of the 1930s. It struck coal fields throughout the United States as mechanization began to perform many of the mining operations in all mines. Natural gas, not coal, became the choice for heating homes; at the same time, electrical generating plants turned to cleaner burning oil. The Illinois fields were unusually hard hit. With the United Mine Workers Union insisting on fair wages and safety measures, southern Illinois coal companies could not compete with coal from areas that did not have to pay for these benefits. Some companies closed their mines in southern Illinois and moved operations to lower-cost areas in the Southeast.

The last great mine disaster happened in 1951 at West Frankfort's New Orient Mine No. 2, when a methane gas explosion killed 119 miners. It was the second most deadly mine disaster in Illinois history. This is the same mine that stood directly in the path of the Tri-State Tornado as it cut its swath across West Frankfort.

By the end of the millennium, coal mining had ceased to be the dominant industry in Little Egypt, although coal reserves are enormous —Illinois still ranks second only to West Virginia in coal reserves.

*   *   *

A curious follow-up—moving along part of the Tri-State path, a second killer tornado struck Gorham and Murphysboro in December, 1957.

It was late Wednesday afternoon on the 18th, and stores were keeping extended hours that week. Shoppers in Murphysboro were out and about. A possible tornado was the last thing on their minds, although thunder had rumbled all day.[6]

A funnel touched down in Missouri, crossed the Mississippi River and damaged half the structures in Gorham, although neither deaths nor serious injuries occurred. For the next seven miles it followed almost exactly the path of the Tri-State, killing one person near Sand Ridge. From the Mississippi River flood plain it crossed the Shawnee Hills and struck Murphysboro around 4:55 P.M. without any warning, killing ten people and injuring 200 in the southeast part of town. A short distance east of town the funnel lifted, but it returned to earth to produce intermittent damage for another thirteen miles in De Soto, Hurst, Bush, and Plumfield. Some of this damage may have been downbursts. Before reaching West Frankfort, it finally dissipated.

This was one of nineteen tornadoes that touched down in southern Illinois that day, one week before Christmas. The temperature had risen unusually high for December—63°F, as a tongue of moist tropical air pushed northward from the Gulf of Mexico ahead of a rapidly advancing cold front. This outbreak killed thirteen people altogether, and 259 suffered severe injuries; property damage ranged between $8 million and $10 million.[7]

CHAPTER 11

Other Great Tornadoes

THE WORD *"TORNADO"* is of uncertain origin. First used in the seventeenth century, British travel writers attributed the term, or terms similar to it, to navigators who described severe thunderstorms off the coast of Africa as "tornadoes." Although it has Spanish or Portuguese roots, the word as we use it is not in either language. *Tronada* means "thunderstorm" in Spanish and the Spanish verb *tornar* means "to turn."

One of the earliest written records of the modern spelling is in a poem from 1788 by British poet William Cowper. In *"Negro Complaints,"* he writes: "Hark—wild tornadoes. Wasting towns, plantations, meadows." Possibly he had the Mississippi Valley in mind when he wrote those lines.

Europeans became aware of the destructive power of tornadoes when they began to settle the North American continent in the sixteenth century. It was not until the great push westward in the latter part of the eighteenth century and nineteenth century that they became the subjects of great discussion and study.

We do have written accounts of a storm that swept out of Missouri and struck Illinois on June 5, 1805, one with some similarities to the Tri-State Tornado 120 years later. Originating in the Missouri Ozarks, it deposited pine boughs on the rich alluvial soil of the American Bottoms of southern Illinois. Those pine boughs grew on trees sixty miles to the west—an area not far from Ellington, Missouri.

The vortex of that storm, a massive black column three quarters of a mile wide, crossed the Mississippi a mile south of the mouth of the Merrimack River. Witnesses reported its passage near the settlement of Albion, about 150 miles east of the Mississippi and sixteen miles west of the Wabash.

Because of the sparse population in the area at that time, whether it reached Indiana—making it a truly tri-state event—cannot be determined. We do know that it left such a wide swath of downed trees in south-central Illinois that this corridor became a major obstacle for travelers for many years.

Illinois governor John Reynolds wrote of it in his memoir, *My Own Times,* published in 1855:

> It was one of those tempests or whirlwinds, which at intervals occurs and desolate the country where it passes. This tornado proceeded with much violence in its course from the southwest to the northeast and crossed the Mississippi about a mile below the mouth of the Merrimack River. It was about three fourths of a mile wide and to that extent it destroyed every living creature, and prostrated every tree in its course. It swept the water out of the Mississippi and lakes in the American Bottom and scattered the fish in every

direction on the dry land. William Blair had a boat moored near it and saw the water of the river raised up in the air and dashed about with the greatest violence.

This tempest passed over the country about one o'clock, and the day before it was clear and pleasant. Persons who saw it informed me that it at first appeared a terrible large black column moving high in the air and whirling round with great violence as it approached. Its size and the terrific roaring attending it increased. It appeared as if innumerable small birds were flying with it in the air; but as it approached nearer, the supposed birds were limbs and branches of trees, propelled with the storm. In the passage of the tempest, perfect and profound darkness prevailed, without any show of light whatever.[1]

A description of the destruction from this storm farther east appeared in an article for a London journal, "The Terrible Tempest of 1805," by John Woods, a visitor to southern Illinois in the second decade of the 19th century. Woods describes the damage that was still apparent in Edwards County, Illinois in 1819. He wrote: "Our road was chiefly through woods, and part of it lay through the hurricane track—that is, where a strong wind some years back opened a passage through the woods a mile in width and some one hundred miles in length. I have heard, from the upper part of the State of Ohio to the Mississippi River and beyond. [The distance from Ohio to the Mississippi River is considerably greater than 100 miles]. This hurricane track is a great harbor for animals and game, as it keeps a large tract unoccupied. But as the hunters generally set fire to the woods in the autumn, many of the trees are burned, but in other places they lie piled high on each other all pointing in the direction of the storm."[2]

Perhaps the great tornado of 1805 was indeed a storm with the dimension of the Tri-State Tornado, but we will never know for sure. There is neither scientific evidence nor newspaper accounts to confirm it. It might have been a series of smaller tornadoes following a continuous path.[3]

Newspapers covered other great storms in the same area in the 19th century for which records are more complete and more reliable. One of the earliest was the Natchez, Mississippi tornado of 1840, the most deadly on record until the Tri-State Tornado. It now is listed as the number two storm on a list of the most deadly American tornadoes on record listed by the U.S. Weather Service.

*   *   *

No. 2: The Natchez Tornado of May 7, 1840

At about 1:45 P.M., a funnel touched down in Louisiana about twenty miles southwest of Natchez, sweeping across cotton fields of rich Delta alluvium destroying many substandard slaves' dwellings before it reached the Mississippi River seven miles below the city. This stretch of the river, downstream from Natchez, flows toward the southwest; thus it was aligned with the storm's path.

At least 269 people died on the river that day. It was crowded with thousands of workers and passengers, transients on flatboats and steamboats. After sweeping the river the tornado left it where the channel changes to the north, and entered Natchez where it killed another forty-five people. The official total of 317 deaths must be approximate since there were rumors that hundreds died on plantations in Louisiana, mostly African-American slaves whose deaths went unreported in the official count. This practice of not listing slaves as casualties in tragedies or accidents was common in the pre-Civil War South. As late as 1925, newspaper lists of dead and injured from the Tri-State Tornado named black victims separately as "negro."[4] (The Natchez Tornado has no Fujita classification because evidence of its intensity is unknown.)

*   *   *

No. 3: The St. Louis Tornado of May 27, 1896

This devastating tornado is rated F4 based on contemporary photographs and newspaper accounts of damage. Although it leveled an area only about twelve miles long, all of its path—eight hundred yards wide—cut through densely settled urban areas of what is now the St. Louis metropolitan area extending from Missouri into Illinois. Downbursts that accompanied the tornado increased the width of the destruction to over a mile. It killed at least 255 and injured more than 1,000. Of the deaths, 137 were in St. Louis and 118 across the river in Illinois. Missing from the record are many deaths of people on the river. Urban property damage far exceeded that caused by other tornadoes in the 19th century.

The loss of life on the Mississippi as the tornado crossed into East St. Louis, Illinois will never be known. The riverfront at St.

Louis was a thriving place with many steamboats and seminomadic shanty boats tied up at the piers. Because of the transient nature of the river population it was difficult to keep track of river men, their names, and the names of family members, friends and relatives. Although few were reported missing on the river, we can assume many were lost but never reported missing.

An eyewitness on the river south of the storm's path supports this assumption. He told a *Post-Dispatch* reporter that "our shanty boat withstood the gale all right, and at our east window we had an excellent view of everything that went down the river. I can say without the least exaggeration that not less than twenty-five of these boats floated down bottom side up. They came from the upper river. Now, just how many persons were under these wrecks is more than anybody knows, and I doubt if we ever will know."[5]

A spectacular lightning show preceded and accompanied the tornado and a witness graphically describes it: "The electrical display at this time was the most vivid ever seen here. Great balls of fire seemed to burst from the clouds, followed by the flash of forked lightning, illuminating the whole of the heavens. At the same time and almost simultaneously there would come a glare from sheets of light. As bright as these were, however, they did not dim the burst of the long, snaky forks of blue electricity. Every color of the rainbow was visible in the electric glare. At the same time the roars of the thunder were appalling."[6]

On March 8, 1871, a smaller but fast-moving tornado—forward speed estimated at 70 mph—had crossed the Mississippi River from St. Louis, Missouri to East St. Louis, Illinois at the same location as the 1896 storm. As in the great 1896 tornado twenty-five years later, considerable damage occurred on the waterfront and the storm destroyed many steamboats and ferries caught out on the river. No deaths occurred in St. Louis, but nine died on the Illinois side. Reacting to this tornado, engineers designed Eads Bridge to be "tornado proof." After the 1896 tornado, a 2-in. by 10-in. plank driven through a 5/16-inch-thick wrought iron plate, was the only damage to this bridge.

* * *

No. 4: The Tupelo Tornado of April 5, 1936

Mention Tupelo, Mississippi and many people will be quick to identify it as the birthplace of Elvis Presley, but ask them about the great tornado there and few will have heard of it. Yet the boy, Elvis, was lucky to have survived that sudden event. It struck Tupelo on a Sunday evening, April 5, 1936, forming out of the same supercell thunderstorm as several others; The first one dropped down near Coffeeville, Mississippi, about sixty miles south-southwest of Tupelo, but the nation's attention focused on the F5 funnel that bore down on the west edge of Tupelo at 8:55 P.M. Moving northeast, it spread destruction and death across the northern half of the town.

The twister struck only a year after the city received the title "First TVA City" (Tennessee Valley Authority) and just as it was beginning its slow recovery from the depths of the Great Depression with an industrial program based on cheap power from the hydro-electric dams on the Tennessee River and its tributaries. The Tennessee River borders the state of Mississippi northeast of Tupelo.

After leveling many well-constructed homes on the west side of town, the tornado then crossed into the northern neighborhoods where dwelled many African Americans. These small, poorly constructed homes were perched on top of a bluff that rose above a backwater slough called Gum Pond. The name "Tupelo" comes from the broad-leafed tupelo gum trees that grew on the swampy soils along the edge of the pond. Many people died when their houses sailed over the bluff down into Gum Pond. Debris from the stricken neighborhoods littered its surface.

Outside the tornado path, in a small house atop the bluffs beyond Gum Pond, a one-year-old Elvis Presley barely escaped death.

Tupelo became the scene of frantic efforts to save the injured. Railroad engineers pulled in 150 boxcars to serve as temporary housing, and wounded survivors filled train cars which backed all the way to Memphis, Tennessee. Civil and electrical engineers came from the TVA to help in the recovery, and more than one thousand WPA workers from neighboring towns arrived to help clean up the town. During the Great Depression the federal government furnished many much-needed jobs to the unemployed, and through the Works Progress Administration these workers were available for national emergencies such as the Tupelo tornado.

The official toll of 216 killed and 700 injured is an approximation. Some estimates place the deaths at 233, but we will never have an accurate count because, although they were counted among the dead, again lists did not record the names of African-American victims, either dead or injured. Since these names did not appear on official death reports, we have no valid lists of black victims.

From the eastern limits of Tupelo the funnel continued northeast across Lee County, finally lifting and dissipating in western

Itawamba County. Its damage trail indicated that it cut a path at least fifteen miles long.

*　*　*

No. 5: Gainsville, Georgia, April 6, 1936

Monday morning and another work week was just beginning as people converged in the center of Gainsville. A few minutes before 8:30 A.M. shopkeepers surrounding the square prepared for the day and numerous high school students hurried through the center of town, a route leading to the school. Early shoppers, clerks, city officials heading toward the courthouse, all converged on the town square as newsboys hawked their papers with the lead story of the Tupelo tragedy the evening before.

At the Cooper pants factory, near the town center, the two hundred mostly young workers arrived on time, happy to have jobs, even low-paying ones. These were hard times indeed. In 1936, Gainsville struggled to survive the steady erosion of its manufacturing base and the collapse of much of its local agricultural base as well. With drought had come general failure of crops in northern Georgia, and boll weevils threatened cotton production.

Shortly before eight-thirty, two tornado funnels approached the city, one from the south-southwest and another from the west. These two twisters joined just west of downtown and, still maintaining two vortices, cut a four-block-wide path through the center of town, striking both the central square and the pants factory.

Wreckage accumulated in the downtown streets to a depth of

ten feet. Havoc reigned in the central square where many buildings collapsed and caught fire, sending flames soaring through the debris. Many trapped victims burned to death. High school students ran into Newman's department store but there was no safety there. Many of them died when the store disintegrated. The Cooper pants factory, a multistoried building, also fell. Fire broke out there; more than seventy of those workers died—the highest tornado-related death toll on record for a single building.

Official statistics list 203 killed and 1,600 injured but many remained unaccounted for. As in other Southern towns, although included in the total number killed or injured, African-American persons did not appear on official lists and it was impossible to follow up on the ultimate fate of those hospitalized.

Beyond the city, the massive double-vortex tornado separated into two distinct funnels and continued northeastward, each on its own separate destructive course, until both finally lifted at the end of their seventeen-mile-long path. A few minutes before the double tornado struck Gainsville, another twister skirted the northern edge of that city and destroyed the Pacolet Mills in suburban New Holland.

Although these tornadoes in northern Georgia originated in a different supercell thunderstorm than those the day before in Mississippi, a single weather system spawned them all. The cold front was part of a cyclone that moved through the middle South on April 5 and 6, traveling eastward at about twenty-five miles per hour. At least a dozen tornadoes developed in the warm, unstable air ahead of it from Arkansas through Tennessee and Mississippi into Georgia and South Carolina. Altogether, these tornadoes, rated from F2 to F5 in intensity, killed more than 400 people and severely injured almost 2,500.

These five most deadly tornadoes in American history each killed more than 200 people. All other killer tornadoes of record caused less than 200 deaths—in most of them only a few people died.

*   *   *

Historic Tornado Outbreaks

Almost as spectacular as individual supertornadoes are the great outbreaks of tornadoes that sometimes occur in the United States. Minor outbreaks take place almost every year, but two great ones stand out—the Palm Sunday outbreak of April 11, 1965, and the greatest of all on April 3-4, 1974.

On Palm Sunday, 1965, thirty-nine tornadoes touched down between 12:45 P.M. and 11:30 P.M. in Iowa, Illinois, Wisconsin, Indiana, Michigan, and Ohio. Although the Weather Bureau issued warnings, nineteen from this marauding band killed a total of 256 persons, and ten of these twisters killed ten or more each. The hardest hit was the northeastern corner of Indiana and the southwestern part of Michigan south of Hillsdale, where two tornadoes followed almost identical paths thirty-five minutes apart. Together, they killed forty-four and injured more than six hundred residents in rural areas, resorts, and small towns. The second most deadly storm of the Palm Sunday outbreak was in Indiana, southeast and east of South Bend. There the death toll was twenty-five.

An amazing display of tornado outbreaks hit the country in 1974. Between the first touchdown in northern Illinois at 1:11 P.M. on April 3, and the final one, at 9:45 A.M., April 4, in North Carolina, a record 148 tornadoes touched down.[7] During this outbreak, tor-

145

nado watches were issued for most of the stricken areas but in spite of them 335 people died and property losses, estimated to have been more than $600 million, set records for a tornado outbreak. We can only speculate on the death toll had no warnings been given.

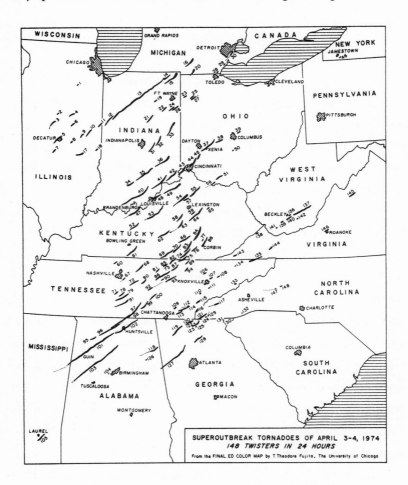

Super outbreak of tornadoes on April 3-4, 1974. In less than twenty-four hours 148 tornadoes touched down from Illinois to North Carolina. The storms are numbered consecutively with the first tornado southwest of Chicago numbered one and the last in North Carolina number 148. (Map by T. Theodore Fujita, The University of Chicago).

Xenia, Ohio, with a population close to twenty-five thousand, suffered the most deaths, thirty-four, when struck by an F5 tornado at about 3:45 P.M. on April 4. This rapidly moving twister touched down about nine miles southwest of Xenia and cut a path through the town, completely demolishing about 300 homes and damaging another 2,100. Two other cities experienced almost as many fatalities as Xenia—Guin, Alabama with thirty people killed, and Tanner, Alabama with twenty-eight.

Length of tornado paths during the outbreak varied from less than a mile to more than 100 miles; the longest path, 121 miles, occurred in the Montecello, Indiana twister. Two other tornadoes traveled more than 100 miles—the Jasper, Alabama twister (103 miles) and the Guin, Alabama storm (102 miles).

*　　*　　*

Tornado Alley

Writing in 1992 about his father's narrow escape in the famous Tupelo tornado, Memphis journalist Gary Moore describes northern Mississippi as lying in "Little Tornado Alley" and further describes the Tri-State Tornado of 1925 as resting in "Little Tornado Alley.[8] J. L. Seed entitled his 1976 article in *See Illinois,* "Tornado Alley—Circa 1925."[9] The term "Tornado Alley," or variants of it, has little meteorological significance; it's really more of a journalistic cliché. It is applied to many areas that have experienced several tornadoes. Numerous "tornado alleys" exist throughout the United States. Placing northern Mississippi in Little Tornado Alley, not just Tornado Alley, illustrates the looseness of the term and its arbitrary use. Even some professional meteorologists use it. A recent book by a respected tornado researcher, *Tornado Alley: Monster Storms of the Great Plains,*[10] is a case in point, although if any part of the country can lay legitimate claim to the term, the Great Plains qualify.

*   *   *

The effectiveness of the national tornado warning system is borne out by the fact that tornado deaths have dropped dramatically since its inception. In 1953, the first year the warning network began to function, the great Worcester, Massachusetts tornado killed ninety-four people. Since then no tornado in the United States has killed that many. Tornado-related deaths had already begun to decline. A peak was reached in the 1920s, in part because of the great death toll from the Tri-State Tornado. After that, average annual fatalities from such storms have decreased continually and dramatically. The last 100-death tornado occurred in 1944, and for the 1990s the annual total killed averaged only fifty-nine. What's even more significant is that this decline coincided with rising population densities in the United States.

Tornado awareness, made possible by rapid media dissemination of tornado alerts, seems an obvious reason for the decline, but how do we account for the drop already underway in the 1930s and 1940s? I believe, along with many other researchers, that the answer lies in the Great Depression when many people abandoned farms in the South and on the Great Plains and began a mass migration to the cities of the North seeking employment and, coincidentally, where the threat of tornadoes is less. Radio played its part when it became affordable for everyone. It became routine to tune into advisories when skies seemed threatening. Now, widespread television storm warnings not only alert our citizens but they educate them about weather phenomena. Weather terminology such as isobars, low pressure areas, fronts, and supercells are now part of the public's vocabulary. Although our knowledge of tornadoes has improved immensely over that in 1925, tornado forecasts remain difficult; the Weather Service does a remarkable job now, choosing to err on the side of safety at the risk of false alarms. They deserve our gratitude.

Notes and References

INTRODUCTION

[1] Statistics for this storm vary between publications. Unless I have otherwise indicated I use figures published in Wilson, J. W. and Stanley A. Changnon, Jr. *Illinois Tornadoes*, Circular 103, Illinois State Water Survey, Urbana, 1971.

CHAPTER 1 – Without Warning

[1] Henry, Alfred J. "Tornadoes of March 18, 1925," *Monthly Weather Review*, April 1925, Vol. 53, No. 4, p. 143.

[2] Today, the Weather Bureau is officially the National Weather Service. It is, as always, the primary weather forecasting and research organization in the United States. In 1940 it shifted to the Department of Commerce through the influence of the emerging aviation industry and ocean shipping.

In 1965 the Bureau, along with the Coast and Geodetic Survey, became a part of the Environmental Science Services Administration (ESSA). In 1970, the National Oceanographic and Atmospheric Administration (NOAA) was created within the Department of Commerce combining the Bureau of Commercial Fisheries, U.S. Weather Bureau, Coast and Geodetic Survey, and Environmental Data Service, National Satellite Center, and research libraries.

CHAPTER 2 – Nature Sets the Stage

[1] Outside the United States, Australia has the greatest number of tornadoes, and like the United States, its topographic barriers run north-south giving full play to air of tropical maritime origin from the north and cooler air from the sub-polar oceans to the south. A source of cold continental air, however, is missing, and perhaps this accounts for the fact that Australian tornadoes are less severe. Argentina also is an area with many tornadoes but less severe ones. There land masses lie equatorward, but cooler oceans do lie to the south.

[2] U.S. Department of Agriculture, Weather Bureau. *Climatological Data, Montana Section,* March 1925.

[3] U.S. Department of Agriculture, Weather Bureau, *Climatological Data, Wyoming Section,* March 1925.

[4] The upper warm, dry air temperatures come from three kites carrying thermometers, sent aloft on March 17, at Broken Arrow, OK, Groesbeck, TX, and Drexel, Mo.

[5] Browning, K. A. "Cellular Structure of Convective Storms." *Meteorological Magazine,* Vol. 90, 1962, pp. 341-349.

[6] Grazulis, Thomas P., *The Tornado, Nature's Ultimate Windstorm,* University of Oklahoma Press, Norman, 2001, p. 33

CHAPTER 3 – Touchdown in Missouri

[1] Pyrtle's story as related by the newspapers failed to report what was actually said, but they reported the action described.

[2] From touchdown to Annapolis its forward speed is estimated to have been seventy-two miles per hour; from Annapolis to Biehl, sixty-seven miles per hour.

[3] Mark Twain [Samuel Clemens], *Life on the Mississippi,* Harper & Brothers Publishers, NY & London, 1874-75.

CHAPTER 4 – The Crossover into Illinois

[1] T. S. Eliot, "Four Quartets," Harcourt, Brace and Co., 1943. Quoted in Horell, C. William, et al. al., *Land Between the Rivers, the Southern Illinois Country*, Southern Illinois University Press, Carbondale, 1973, p. 121.

[2] Flint, Timothy. *Recollections of the Last Ten Years* (1826), as quoted in Horell, p. 115.

[3] St. Louis Post-Dispatch, March 20, 1925, p. 1.

[4] The Fujita (F) scale of tornado intensity is given at the beginning of this book.

[5] Grazulis, Thomas P. *The Tornado, Nature's Ultimate Windstorm,* University of Oklahoma Press, Norman, 2001, p. 119.

[6] St. Louis Post-Dispatch, March 20, 1925, p. 2.

[7] St. Louis Post-Dispatch, March 20, 1925, p. 2.

[8] Jackson County, Illinois Historical Society. Transcription of a recording of a meeting to discuss the Murphysboro Tornado (No date). From the Illinois State Library, Springfield.

[9] The Daily Independent (Murphysboro, Illinois), March 18, 1926, Special Edition, Section 2. p. 7.

CHAPTER 5 – Murphysboro

[1] Jones, P. Michael, Robert R. Morefield, and Clifton Swafford, *Murphysboro, Illinois—150 Years*, 1843-1993. Jackson County Historical Society, 1994, p. 39.

[2] St. Louis Post-Dispatch, March 20, 1925, p. 4.

[3] St. Louis Post-Dispatch, March 22, 1925, p. 2,

[4] Daily Independent (Murphysboro, Illinois) Special Edition, March 18, 1926, Section 2, p. 9.

[5] Daily Independent (Murphysboro, Illinois) Special Edition, March 18, 1926, Section 2, p. 9.

6 St. Louis Post-Dispatch, March 19, 1925, p. 4.

7 St. Louis Post-Dispatch, March 19, 1925, p. 4.

8 Seed, J. L. "Tornado Alley—Circa 1925," *See Illinois,* March-April, 1976, Vol. 2, No. 5, p. 5.

9 *The Illinois State Register,* March 21, 1925, pp. 1, 7.

CHAPTER 6 – De Soto

1 Most likely Hewitt worked as an insurance agent and he had come to write up a policy for the twins. Agents visited homes for this purpose and to collect premiums.

2 St. Louis Post-Dispatch, March 21, 1925, p. 1.

3 It was not unusual for survivors to estimate that the tornado lasted as long as fifteen minutes.

4 *St. Louis Post-Dispatch,* March 21, 1925, p. 1.

5 *St. Louis Post-Dispatch,* March 21, 1925, p. 1.

6 *The New York Times,* March 19, 1925.

7 This comparison reflects the prevalence and importance of trains during the first half of the twentieth century.

8 St. Louis Post Dispatch, March 20, 1925, Evening Edition, p. 8.

9 St. Louis Post Dispatch, March 20, 1925, Evening Edition, p. 8.

CHAPTER 7 – West Frankfort

1 In 1925, the world's largest coal mine was reported to be in the USSR. This ranking was based on the coal brought to the surface in one day.

2 An electrical sump pump pumps water that collects in a special pit—the sump—out of the mine.

3 Information on thickness of coal seams that determine the height of mine ceilings from Illinois State Geological Survey, *Directory of Coal Mines in Illinois, Franklin County, May 2000.*

[4] *St. Louis Post-Dispatch,* March 20, 1925, p. 1.

[5] *St. Louis Post-Dispatch,* March 20, 1925, 1.

[6] *St. Louis Post-Dispatch,* March 20, 1925, p. 1.

[7] Baumhoff did not list the names of his companions on the trip to southern Illinois, but we can assume he was accompanied by O'Neal since O'Neal's byline appeared over stories from De Soto in the Post-Dispatch the next day.

[8] Baumhoff, Richard, *St. Louis Post-Dispatch,* March 21, 1925,. p. 1.

[9] Baumhoff. Ibid.

[10] Baumhoff. Ibid.

[11] Baumhoff. Ibid.

[12] Wilson, J. W. and S. A. Changnon, Jr., *Illinois Tornadoes.* Illinois State Water Survey. Circular 103, 1971, pp. 32-38.

CHAPTER 8 – Parrish and Eastern Illinois

[1] *St. Louis Post-Dispatch,* March 20, 1925.

[2] Ibid.

[3] Ibid.

[4] Ibid.

[5] New York Times, March 20, 1925.

[6] Ibid.

[7] American Heritage, *My Brush With History,* Black Dog and Levanthall, New York 2001, pp. 26-27.

CHAPTER 9 – Indiana

[1] *St. Louis Post-Dispatch,* March 20, 1925, p. 8.

[2] Chicago Tribune [Final Edition] March 23, 1925, p. 1.

[3] *St. Louis Post-Dispatch,* [Evening Edition], March 20, 1925, p. 3.

[4] Princeton Clarion, March 19, 1925, P. 1.

[5] Princeton Clarion, March 19, 1925, p. 1.

[6] The Indianapolis Times, March 20, 1925, p. 14.

[7] Princeton Clarion, March 19, 1925, p. 2.

[8] Princeton Clarion, March 19, 1925, p. 2.

[9] Indianapolis Star, March 19, 1925, p. 1.

[10] Princeton Clarion, March 20, 1925, p. 8.

CHAPTER 10 – The Aftermath

[1] The New York Times, March 22, 1925, p. 1.

[2] Daily Republican (Marion, Illinois), March 20, 1925, p. 2. As quoted in Felknor (1992), p. 83-84.

[3] Daily Independent (Murphysboro, Illinois), March 23, 1925, p. 7-8.

[4] Daily Independent (Murphysboro, Illinois) Special Edition, March 18, 1926.

[5] Wilson, John W. and Stanley A. Changnon, Jr. *Illinois Tornadoes,* Illinois State Water Survey, Urbana. 1971, circular 103, pp. 35-36.

[6] *Southern Illinoisan.* December 19, 1957, p. 1.

[7] Wilson, J. W. and S. A. Changnon, Jr., *Illinois Tornadoes.* Illinois State Water Survey. Urbana, 1971, Circular 103, pp. 39-41.

CHAPTER 11 – Other Great Tornadoes

[1] Reynolds, John. *My Own Times.* Chicago Historical Society. 1879 (Reprint University Microfilms, Ann Arbor, 1968), pp. 107-08.

[2] Joy, Judith. "The Great Tornado of 1925," *Illinois Magazine,* March 1976, pp. 27-28.

[3] Joy, Judith. "The Great Tornado of 1925," *Illinois Magazine,* March 1976, p. 28.

[4] In 1925, the newspapers identified blacks but did not capitalize "negro."

5 *St. Louis Post-Dispatch,* June 1, 1896.

6 *St. Louis Post-Dispatch,* June 3, 1896 (Special Illustrated Tornado Edition).

7 Fujita's first estimate of tornadoes touching down during the outbreak (148) was later revised to 147; on reevaluation of the data, one of the storms was reclassified as a violent wind but not a tornado. The original 148 still is listed in the official figures.

8 Moore, Gary. "The Great Tupelo Tornado," *Weatherwise,* October/November 1992, pp. 16-19.

9 Seed, J. L. "Tornado Alley—Cerca 1925," *see Illinois.* March-April, 1976, pp. 2-7.

10 Bluestein, Howard B. *Tornado Alley: Monster Storms of the Great Plains,* Oxford University Press, New York, 1999.

FURTHER READING

Bluestein, Howard B. *Tornado Alley: Monster Storms of the Great Plains.* Oxford University Press, New York, 1999. An up-to-date account of recent advances in the study of tornadoes by one of the foremost tornado experts in the country who furnishes many fine illustrations and photographs.

Felknor, Peter S. *The Tri-State Tornado: The Story of America's Greatest Disaster.* Iowa State University Press, Ames, 1992. In the late 1980s, Felknor retraced the path of the Tri-State Tornado, interviewing along the way elderly citizens who were school children when the tornado struck. The book is filled with stories of their recollections.

Flora, Snowden D. *Tornadoes of the United States.* University of Oklahoma Press, Norman, 1954. This classic work, now out of print but readily available in libraries, is the first summary of great tornadoes throughout American history.

Grazulis, Thomas P. *The Tornado, Nature's Ultimate Windstorm.* University of Oklahoma Press, Norman, 2000. For the general reader this is a complete coverage of tornadoes available in one volume. Highly recommended.

Hughs, Patrick. *A Century of the Weather Service, 1870-1970.* Gordon and Breach, Science Publishers, Inc., New York, 1970. Out of print but available in libraries. Its chronological listing of important events in the history of the Weather Service is particularly valuable.

Jones, Michael P., Robert R. Morefield, and Clifton Swafford. (Vickie Frost, Editor). *Murphysboro, Illinois, 150 Years: A Pictorial History, 1843-1993.* The Jackson County Historical Society, Murphysboro, IL, 1994. A history of my hometown with a particularly good section—especially the photographs—on the Tri-State Tornado.

Kessler, Edwin, editor. *The Thunderstorm in Human Affairs (Second Edition)*. University of Oklahoma Press, Norman, 1983. Various specialists in meteorology and related fields address thunderstorms and related subjects, including tornadoes.

Mogil, H. Michael. *Tornadoes*. Voyager Press (World Life Library). Stillwater, NM, 2001. A book on tornadoes for the general reader with excellent photographs and diagrams that depict the meteorology of a tornado.

Mowat, Farley, *The Serpent's Coil: An Incredible Story of Hurricane-Battered Ships and Heroic Men Who Fought to Save Them*. The Lyons Press, New York, 2001. This true story is about another kind of windstorm, the hurricane, written by a master storyteller. Well worth a read.

Stewart, George R. *Storm*. Random House—The Modern Library, New York, 1941, 1947. A fictional account of a middle latitude cyclonic storm that struck the California coast. A classic.

Zebrowski, Ernest, Jr. *Perils of a Restless Planet: Scientific Perspectives on Natural Disasters*. Cambridge University Press, Cambridge, UK, 1997. More technical but written for the general reader, the book delves into the causes of natural catastrophes. The section on wind and its destructive potential is particularly instructive.

BIBLIOGRAPHY

Books and Articles Consulted

Abbey, Robert F. Jr. and T. Theodore Fujita. "Tornadoes: The Tornado Outbreak of 3-4 April 1974." In Edwin Kessler, edit. *The Thunderstorm in Human Affairs*. University of Oklahoma Press, Norman, 1983, pp. 37-62.

Alinsky, Saul. *John L. Lewis: An Unauthorized Biography*. G. P. Putnam's Sons, New York, 1949.

American Heritage Editors. *My Brush With History*. Black Dog and Levanthall, Pub., New York, 2001.

Atkinson, William. *The Next New Madrid Earthquake: A Survival Guide to the Midwest*. Southern Illinois Univ. Press, Carbondale, 1989.

Bates, F. C. "Tornadoes in the Central United States." *Transactions Kansas Academy of Science*. Vol. 65, No. 3, 1963, pp. 215-246.

Bluestein, Howard B. *Tornado Alley: Monster Storms of the Great Plains*, Oxford University Press, New York, 1999.

Carrier, Lois. *Illinois: Crossroads of a Continent*. Univ. of Illinois Press, Urbana, 1993.

Chicago Tribune. Microfilm of issues from March 17 through March 31, 1925.

Childres, William. *Out of the Ozarks*. Southern Illinois Univ. Press. Carbondale, 1987.

Christian Science Monitor, The. Microfilm of issues from March 18 through March 31, 1925.

Church, C., et al., eds. *The Tornado: its Structure, Dynamics, Prediction, and Hazards*. American Geophysical Union, Geophysical Monograph 79. Washington, D. C., 1993.

Clemons, Samuel L. [Mark Twain]. *Life of the Mississippi.* Harpers and Brothers Publisher, New York, 1911.

Corlis, William R. *Tornados* [sic.], *Dark days, Anomalous Precipitation, and Related Weather Phenomena.* The Sourcebook Project, Glen Arm, MD, 1983.

Daily Independent. (Murphysboro, IL). Microfilm of issues from March 19 through March 31, 1925 and March 18, 1926.

Des Moines Tribune. Microfilm of issues from March 18 through March 31, 1925.

Dorson, Richard M. *Buying the Wind: Regional Folklore in the United States.* The Univ. of Chicago Press, Chicago, IL, 1964.

Eagleman, Joe R. *Severe and Unusual Weather,* 2nd edit. Trimedia Publishing Co. Lenexa, KS, 1990.

Felknor, Peter S. *The Tri-State Tornado, The Story of America's Greatest Tornado Disaster.* Iowa State University Press, Ames, 1992.

Flora, Snowden D. *Tornadoes of the United States.* Univ. of Oklahoma Press, Norman, 1954.

Foley, William E., *The Genesis of Missouri: From Wilderness Outpost to Statehood.* Univ. of Missouri Press, Colombia, 1989.

Fujita, T. T. and B. E. Smith. "Aerial Survey and Photography of Tornado and Microburst Damage," in C. Church, et al. *The Tornado: Its Structure, Dynamics, Prediction, and Hazards.* Geophysical Monograph 79. American Geophysical Union, Washington, D. C., 1993, pp. 479-493.

Galway, Joseph G. "J. P. Finley: The First Severe Storms Forecaster." *Bulletin American Meteorological Society,* 1985, Vol. 66. pp. 1380-95; 1506-10.

Gerlach, Russel L. *Settlement Patterns in Missouri.* Univ. of Missouri Press, Colombia, 1986.

Grazulis, Thomas P. *The Tornado, Nature's Ultimate Windstorm.* Univ. of Oklahoma Press, 2000.

Horrel, William C., Henry Dan Piper, and John W. Voigt. *Land Between the Rivers: The Southern Illinois Country.* Southern Illinois Univ. Press, Carbondale, 1973.

Hughes, Patrick. *A Century of Weather Service, 1870-1970.* Gordon and Breach, Science Publishers, Inc. New York, 1970.

Illinois State Journal. Springfield. Microfilm for issues of March 19 through March 31, 1925.

Imhoff, Edgar Allen. *Always of Home: A Southern Illinois Childhood.* Southern Illinois University Press, Carbondale, 1993.

Indianapolis Star, The. Microfilm for issues of March 18 through March 31, 1925.

Indianapolis Times, The. Microfilm of issues from March 18 through March 31, 1925.

Jones, Michael P., Morefield, Robert R., Swafford, Clifton; Frost, Vickie (editor). *Murphysboro, Illinois, 150 Years: A Pictorial History, 1843-1993.* The Jackson County Historical Society, Murphysboro, IL, 1994.

Joy, Judith, "The Great Tornado of 1925." *Illinois Magazine,* March 1978. pp. 8-30.

Junger, Sebastian, *The Perfect Storm: A True Story of Men Against the Sea.* (Paperback Printing) Harper Torch, New York, 2000.

Kessler, Edwin, editor. *The Thunderstorm in Human Affairs* (Second Edition). Univ. of Oklahoma Press, Norman, 1983.

Korson, George. *Coal Dust on the Fiddle: Songs and Stories of the Bituminous Industry.* Folklore Associates, Inc., Hatboro, PA, 1965.

Lantz, Herman R. *People of Coal Town.* Columbia Univ. Press, New York, 1958.

Larson, Erik. *Isaac's Storm: A Man, a Time, and the Deadliest Hurricane in History.* Vintage Books, New York, 2000.

Ludlum, David M. *The Weather Factor,* Houghton Mifflin Co., Boston, 1984.

Massey, Ellen Gray (editor). *Bittersweet Country.* Univ. of Oklahoma Press, Norman, 1986.

Mc Dermott, John Francis. *The Lost Panoramas of the Mississippi.* The Univ. of Chicago Press, 1958.

McNeil, W. K. *Ozark Country.* University Press of Mississippi, Jackson, 1995.

Mogil, H. Michael. *Tornadoes.* Voyager Press (World Life Library). Stillwater, NM, 2001.

Morris, Lawrence. *The Plight of the Bituminous Coal Miner.* University of Pennsylvania Press, Philadelphia, 1934.

Mowat, Farley, *The Serpent's Coil: An Incredible Story of Hurricane-Battered Ships and the Heroic Men Who Fought to Save Them.* The Lyons Press, New York, 2001.

New York Times. Microfilm of issues from March 18 through March 31, 1925.

Penick, James, Jr. *The New Madrid Earthquakes of 1811-1812.* Univ. of Missouri Press, 1976.

Princeton Clarion. Microfilm for issues from March 18 through March 31, 1925.

Raban, Jonathan. *Old Glory: An American Voyage.* Simon and Schuster, New York, 1981.

Rafferty, Milton D. *Missouri: A Geography.* Westview Press, Boulder, CO, 1983.

Rafferty, Milton D. *Historical Atlas of Missouri.* Univ. of Oklahoma Press, Norman, 1982.

Russell, Herbert K. *A Southern Illinois Album. Farm Security Administration Photographs. 1936-1943.* Southern Illinois Univ. Press, Carbondale, 1990.

Seed, J. L. "Tornado Alley—Circa 1925." See Illinois, April 1976, pp. 2-7.

Stanford, John L. *Tornado: Accounts of Tornadoes in Iowa.* Iowa State University Press, Ames, 1977.

Steward, Dick. *Duels and the Roots of Violence in Missouri,* University of Missouri Press, Columbia, 2000.

Stewart, George R. *Storm.* Modern Library, New York, 1947.

St. Louis Post-Dispatch. Microfilm of issues from March 17 through March 31, 1925.

Twain, Mark [Samuel L. Clemons]. *Life on the Mississippi.* Harpers and Brothers Publisher, New York, 1911.

Western Society of Engineers. "Report on Effects of Tornado of March 18, 1925." *Journal of the Western Society of Engineers. Technical Papers.* September, 1925, pp. 373-395.

Whitnaw, Donald R. *A History of the United States Weather Bureau.* Univ. of Illinois Press, Urbana, 1961.

Wieck, Edward E. *Preventing Fatal Explosions in Coal Mines.* Russel Sage Foundation New York, 1942.

Wilson, J. W. and S. A. Changnon, Jr., *Illinois Tornadoes.* Illinois State Water Survey. Circular 103, 1971. pp. 32-41.

Wilson, William E. *Indiana, A History.* Indiana Univ. Press, Bloomington, 1966.

Wolf, John Quincy. *Life in the Leatherwoods.* Memphis State Univ. Press, Memphis, TN, 1974.

Zebrowski, Ernest, Jr. *Perils of a Restless Planet: Scientific Perspectives on Natural Disasters.* Cambridge Univ. Press, Cambridge, UK, 1997.

Index

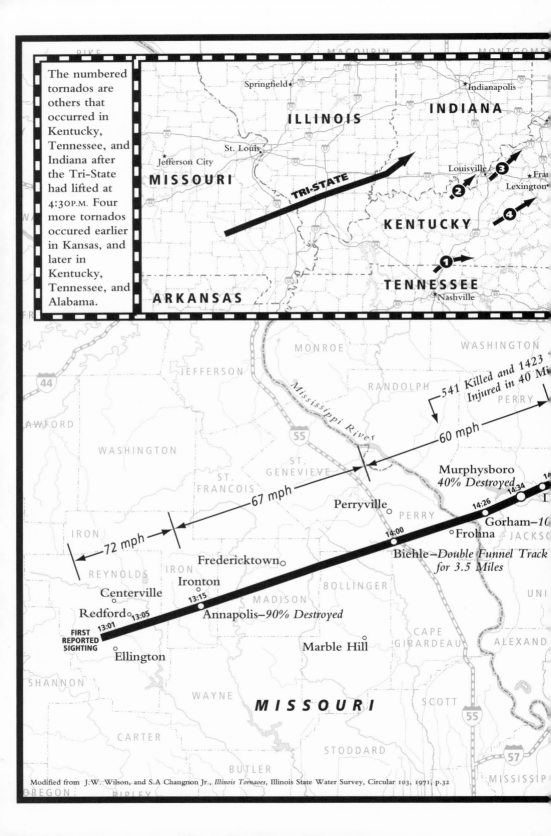

The numbered tornados are others that occurred in Kentucky, Tennessee, and Indiana after the Tri-State had lifted at 4:30 P.M. Four more tornados occured earlier in Kansas, and later in Kentucky, Tennessee, and Alabama.

Springfield

INDIANA

Indianapolis

ILLINOIS

St. Louis

Jefferson City

MISSOURI

TRI-STATE

Louisville ③
② Fran
Lexington ④

KENTUCKY

①

TENNESSEE
Nashville

ARKANSAS

MONROE   WASHINGTON

JEFFERSON   RANDOLPH   PERRY

541 Killed and 1423
Injured in 40 Mi

Mississippi River

60 mph

WASHINGTON

ST.
GENEVIEVE

Murphysboro
40% Destroyed

ST.
FRANCIS   Perryville○   PERRY   14:34

67 mph   14:26

Gorham—10

IRON   14:00   Frohna

72 mph   Fredericktown○   Biehle—Double Funnel Track
                                           for 3.5 Miles

REYNOLDS   IRON   Ironton○   BOLLINGER

Centerville○   13:15   MADISON

Redford○ 13:05   Annapolis—90% Destroyed   CAPE

FIRST   13:01   Marble Hill○   GIRARDEAU   ALEXAND
REPORTED
SIGHTING   ○Ellington

SHANNON   WAYNE   MISSOURI   SCOTT

CARTER   STODDARD   57

BUTLER   MISSISSIP

Modified from J.W. Wilson, and S.A Changnon Jr., *Illinois Tornaoes*, Illinois State Water Survey, Circular 103, 1971, p.32